THE
PUPPET MASTERS PLAYBOOK

Unveiling Covert Manipulation Techniques

By
JONATHAN GRAVES

Copyright © 2025

All rights reserved.

No part of this book may be copied, reproduced, stored in a retrieval system, or transmitted in any form or by any means—electronic, mechanical, photocopying, recording, or otherwise—without the prior written permission of the publisher, except in the case of brief quotations for review purposes.

This book is intended for informational and educational purposes only. It is not a substitute for professional legal, psychological, or medical advice. The author and publisher disclaim any liability for the misuse or misinterpretation of the content provided.

Any unauthorized distribution, reproduction, or resale of this material is strictly prohibited and may result in legal action.

INTRODUCTION

INTRODUCTION: The Invisible Hand of Influence — 1

CHAPTER 1: The Four Laws of Covert Manipulation — 3

   Perception is Reality — 3
   People Are Predictable — 7
   Subtlety Wins: Why Obvious Manipulation Fails — 12
   Control the Frame, Control the Outcome — 16

CHAPTER 2: The Science of Suggestion – How to Implant Ideas — 23

   The Subconscious Planting Method — 23
   Indirect Influence: Making People Think It Was Their Idea — 28
   Repetition & Priming: The Psychological Trojan Horse — 32
   The Zeigarnik Effect: How Unfinished Thoughts Create Obsession — 37

CHAPTER 3: Psychological Tricks for Influence — 43

   Mirroring: The Fastest Way to Build Trust — 43
   The Illusion of Certainty: How Confidence Overrides Truth — 48
   Anchoring: Creating Emotional Associations for Influence — 52
   The Power of Strategic Silence — 57
   The Yes-Ladder Technique: Creating a Pattern of Agreement — 62

CHAPTER 4: Social Engineering – The Tactics of Con Artists & Intelligence Agencies — 67

   The Pretext Method: Creating Stories That Build Trust Instantly — 67
   The Illusion of Morality: How Ethics Are Used to Manipulate — 72
   The Illusion of Consensus: How Group Pressure Shapes Decisions — 76
   Emotional Hijacking: Controlling Actions by Triggering Feelings — 80

CHAPTER 5: The Dark Side – How Manipulation is Used in the Real World — 87

   Advertising & Marketing: The Science of Consumer Control — 87
   Politics & Propaganda: Shaping Public Opinion — 92
   Social Media: The Algorithmic Manipulation Machine — 97
   Personal Relationships: Subtle Control in Everyday Interactions — 102

CHAPTER 6: How to Defend Yourself Against Manipulation   109

   Recognizing Covert Influence: The Hidden Red Flags   109
   Becoming "Unmanipulatable": Strengthening Psychological Resistance   114
   The Mental Autonomy Blueprint: Staying in Control of Your Own Mind   119

CHAPTER 7: The 7-Day Influence Experiment   125

   Day 1-2: Practicing Subtle Suggestion   125
   Day 3-4: Building Trust and Influence with Mirroring & Priming   128
   Day 5-6: Anchoring & Emotional Triggers in Action   132
   Day 7: Testing Full Influence Techniques in a Real Situation   137

FINAL WORDS: Mastering Influence and Protecting Your Mind   143

INTRODUCTION
THE INVISIBLE HAND OF INFLUENCE

What if you could make people agree with you—without them realizing they were being influenced? What if your words could implant ideas, steer emotions, and shape reality itself? Influence is not about forcing someone into submission. The most powerful manipulators do not argue, command, or coerce. They create an environment where their targets willingly comply, believing their decisions are entirely their own.

We live in an age of hidden persuasion, where those who understand the mechanics of the human mind dictate the choices of those who do not. From the way advertisements shape consumer desires to the subtle psychological triggers embedded in political speeches, nearly everything we see, hear, and read is designed to guide our perception. The world is not controlled by force; it is controlled by suggestion. If you have ever agreed to something and later wondered why, if you have ever found yourself emotionally hooked by a speech, an argument, or an idea, then you have felt the weight of unseen influence pressing down on you.

The truth is simple: manipulation is everywhere. It happens in personal relationships, corporate boardrooms, media narratives, and even casual social interactions. Some wield it to gain power, some to persuade, some to deceive. Others fall victim to its effects without realizing it, blindly accepting the realities that have been carefully constructed around them. The difference between those who influence and those who are influenced comes down to awareness. Those who recognize the invisible strings pulling at their decisions can choose whether to resist or embrace them. Those who remain unaware simply become puppets.

This book is not about cheap tricks or superficial persuasion tactics. It is about understanding the deeper psychological frameworks that govern human behavior—

how thoughts are implanted, how emotions override reason, how repetition builds truth, and how authority bends perception. It explores the covert strategies used by master manipulators, social engineers, and elite persuaders. More importantly, it teaches you how to recognize when these tactics are being used against you. Knowledge of influence is power, and that power can be wielded for personal growth, leadership, and persuasion—or for deception, control, and manipulation. The ethical line is yours to define.

A word of caution: the techniques in this book are powerful. They can be used to protect yourself from manipulation, to strengthen your ability to influence others ethically, or to gain an advantage in business, negotiation, and social dynamics. But in the wrong hands, these same strategies can be weaponized to exploit, deceive, and coerce. Influence is a double-edged sword—those who misuse it often find themselves trapped by their own illusions of control.

This book does not judge, but it does warn: once you understand how manipulation works, you will start seeing it everywhere. In conversations, in headlines, in the smallest choices you make daily. You will no longer simply react—you will begin to analyze, question, and strategically position yourself in every interaction. The world will not look the same once you see the hidden levers behind persuasion. The question is, are you ready to see it?

CHAPTER 1
THE FOUR LAWS OF COVERT MANIPULATION

Before mastering the art of manipulation, you must first understand the fundamental laws that govern influence. These principles shape how people perceive the world, make decisions, and respond to external stimuli. Covert manipulation isn't about brute force or direct control—it's about subtly shifting perception in a way that feels natural to the target. The key to success lies in mastering perception, suggestion, and emotional influence without the subject ever realizing they are being guided.

Perception is Reality

Human beings don't perceive reality directly; they interpret it through a mental filter shaped by past experiences, emotions, expectations, and biases. Two people can witness the same event and come away with completely different understandings of what occurred. This is because perception is not a reflection of objective reality but a constructed version of it.

The ability to manipulate someone's perception is one of the most powerful tools of covert influence. If you control how someone sees a situation, you control how they react to it. Whether in business, relationships, politics, or social interactions, those who shape perception dictate decisions without force or direct persuasion.

The Illusion of Objectivity

Most people believe they are rational decision-makers who assess the world logically and base their conclusions on facts. However, modern psychology has repeatedly demonstrated that human thinking is anything but objective. Biases distort reasoning, emotions override logic, and environmental influences shift beliefs without conscious awareness.

Take, for example, **confirmation bias**—the tendency to seek out and believe information that supports pre-existing ideas while ignoring or dismissing evidence to the contrary. This bias explains why political debates rarely change minds, why loyal customers continue buying from a brand despite superior alternatives, and why people become entrenched in belief systems that may be factually incorrect.

Another common cognitive distortion is the **availability heuristic**, where people judge the likelihood of an event based on how easily they can recall similar occurrences. If a person recently saw news reports of a plane crash, they will irrationally overestimate the risk of flying, even though statistics show that flying remains one of the safest modes of transport. Manipulators take advantage of this by controlling the flow of information—by selectively presenting certain facts while omitting others, they can shape a target's risk perception, fear level, and decision-making process.

One of the most famous experiments demonstrating this effect was conducted by Elizabeth Loftus. In her studies on memory, participants who were asked leading questions about an event often misremembered details based on the phrasing of the question. When asked, *"How fast was the car going when it smashed into the other vehicle?"*, participants estimated higher speeds than when the question used the word *"hit"* instead. The language alone reshaped their perception of the event.

The key takeaway? Reality doesn't matter—perception does. And perception is highly malleable.

Controlling Perception to Control Behavior

Once someone's perception of a situation is manipulated, their decisions naturally follow. This principle is heavily studied in **behavioral economics**, which explores how seemingly insignificant changes in presentation alter human choices.

A prime example is the **framing effect**. Imagine you are given these two options:

- *"This procedure has a 90% survival rate."*
- *"This procedure has a 10% chance of death."*

Logically, both statements convey the same information. However, studies show that people are significantly more likely to accept the procedure when it is framed in terms of survival rather than death. The human brain does not process numbers in a vacuum—it reacts emotionally to context.

This principle is applied everywhere, from advertising to political rhetoric:

- **Sales tactics:** A product is marketed as "available for only $99.99" instead of "costs $100."
- **Political messaging:** A law is framed as "protecting national security" rather than "increasing surveillance."
- **Workplace influence:** A manager says, "We have the opportunity to improve efficiency" rather than "We're fixing mistakes."

People make decisions based on their perception of reality, not reality itself. The way a message is framed determines how it is received.

The Role of Emotion in Perception

Emotions dictate how individuals interpret events. A person in a positive emotional state will see neutral situations as favorable, while someone in a negative state will perceive those same situations as threats.

This is why **emotion priming** is such a powerful tool in manipulation. By influencing a person's emotional state before presenting information, you can dramatically alter how they interpret that information.

For example, interrogators build rapport before asking crucial questions. Once a suspect feels comfortable, they are more likely to answer honestly and less likely to recognize manipulative questioning tactics. Similarly, in sales, a skilled negotiator will first engage in small talk, crack a joke, or offer a compliment to create a positive atmosphere before making a pitch.

Emotional control is also why **fear-based persuasion** is so effective. News networks use this constantly—by instilling fear before presenting information, they ensure that the audience reacts emotionally rather than rationally. A fearful mind is more susceptible to suggestion, making it easier to shape opinions.

Shaping Reality Through Repetition

The **illusory truth effect** states that the more often something is heard, the more likely it is to be believed, even if it is false. Repetition creates familiarity, and the brain equates familiarity with truth.

This is why advertising, political campaigns, and propaganda rely on **consistent messaging** to influence public perception. A 1977 study by Hasher, Goldstein, and Toppino demonstrated that statements repeated multiple times were perceived as more truthful than statements only heard once, regardless of accuracy.

Repetition is most effective when combined with **credibility and social proof**. When a message is repeated across multiple sources—especially from authoritative or trusted figures—it solidifies as truth. This is how social media algorithms manipulate perception: by showing users content they already engage with, they reinforce existing beliefs, creating ideological echo chambers.

This technique can be applied in everyday interactions:

- **In personal influence:** Repeating key phrases during conversations subtly imprints ideas in someone's mind.
- **In workplace dynamics:** A leader who repeatedly emphasizes a company's "mission" fosters employee loyalty.
- **In persuasion:** A negotiator who frequently restates the benefits of a deal increases the likelihood of acceptance.

Application: How to Reshape Perception

Master manipulators don't need to change reality—only how people perceive it. To reshape perception, follow these five principles:

1. **Frame the narrative:** Present information in a way that emphasizes benefits while minimizing drawbacks.
2. **Control exposure:** Limit contradictory information while reinforcing key messages.
3. **Engage emotions:** Arouse specific feelings to shape interpretation.
4. **Use repetition:** Repeat ideas in different forms to solidify belief.
5. **Leverage authority and social proof:** Support claims with credible sources and group consensus.

By mastering these techniques, you can subtly influence others without them realizing they are being guided. The key to covert manipulation is making people believe they are acting on their own free will while, in reality, they are following a carefully crafted path of perception.

People Are Predictable

Every person believes they are unique in their decision-making, but in reality, human behavior follows predictable patterns. People act in accordance with their past experiences, subconscious biases, and psychological conditioning. When you understand these patterns, you gain the ability to anticipate how someone will respond in a given situation—allowing you to subtly influence their decisions before they even realize it.

The predictability of human behavior is why advertisers, politicians, and con artists can manipulate vast numbers of people with remarkable accuracy. They don't need to control every individual's thoughts directly; they only need to create the right conditions that lead to expected outcomes.

Understanding **why** people make predictable choices is the foundation of covert manipulation. Once you recognize that humans are not as independent as they believe, you can control situations without resistance.

The Science of Behavioral Patterns

Psychologists and neuroscientists have spent decades studying how people make decisions, revealing that most choices are **not** the result of conscious thought. Instead, they are driven by **habit loops, emotional triggers, and automatic responses** shaped by past experiences.

One of the most influential studies on behavior was conducted by psychologist B.F. Skinner in the mid-20th century. His research on **operant conditioning** demonstrated that behavior could be reinforced through **rewards and punishments**. When an action produces a positive outcome, people are likely to repeat it; when it results in discomfort, they avoid it. This principle is the basis for many forms of manipulation, from sales tactics to social engineering.

For example:

- **Gamification:** Apps and social media platforms reward engagement with dopamine-triggering notifications, making people return repeatedly.
- **Fear-based persuasion:** Politicians use fear of loss to steer public opinion. When people are afraid, they default to predictable defensive behavior.
- **Interpersonal influence:** A manipulator reinforces behaviors they want by providing positive feedback while subtly discouraging resistance through disapproval or subtle punishment.

The **key insight** here is that most people repeat behaviors without critically analyzing them. By recognizing their existing patterns, you can predict their future actions.

The Role of Habit in Predictability

People often believe they make rational, conscious choices throughout the day. However, studies show that nearly **45% of daily behaviors are habitual**—meaning they occur automatically, without real thought. These habits shape how people react in social situations, how they process information, and even how they make financial and relationship decisions.

Manipulators exploit habitual behavior in two key ways:

1. By reinforcing existing habits to guide people toward a desired outcome.

- Example: A salesperson mirrors a customer's buying routine, subtly encouraging them to stay within familiar patterns rather than question the purchase.

2. By disrupting habits to create a moment of vulnerability.

- Example: A scam artist changes a target's normal environment—such as calling unexpectedly or showing up unannounced—forcing them into unfamiliar territory where they are more susceptible to influence.

Breaking a habit makes people **more receptive to external guidance**. This is why life transitions—moving to a new city, starting a new job, or experiencing emotional turmoil—are the moments when people are most vulnerable to manipulation.

Anticipating Actions Before They Happen

Once you understand that behavior follows patterns, you can **predict how people will respond before they act**.

Here are three proven psychological triggers that drive behavior in predictable ways:

1. The Commitment Principle

People strive for consistency in their actions and beliefs. Once they commit to an idea or decision, they resist changing their minds, even when presented with contradictory evidence.

- **How to exploit it:** Get someone to agree to a small action, then escalate the commitment gradually.
- This is known as the **foot-in-the-door technique**—once a person takes one step in a certain direction, they are more likely to continue down that path.
- **Example:** A car salesman first asks a customer to take a test drive (a small commitment). Once they agree, they become psychologically invested in the idea of owning the car, making them more likely to buy.

2. The Authority Effect

People instinctively obey perceived authority figures, even when the orders go against their personal values. This was famously demonstrated in the **Milgram experiment**, where participants obeyed instructions to administer (fake) electric shocks to another person, simply because an authority figure told them to.

- **How to exploit it:** Position yourself as a knowledgeable or authoritative source. People are more likely to follow your lead if they perceive you as having expertise or higher status.
- **Example:** Doctors, police officers, and CEOs are given instant credibility in conversations. Even subtle signs of authority—such as dressing well, using confident body language, or speaking in a calm and controlled manner—increase compliance.

3. The Scarcity Principle

People assign more value to things they perceive as rare or limited. This instinct is a survival mechanism—when resources are scarce, they become more desirable.

- **How to exploit it:** Create urgency by suggesting that an opportunity is limited in time or availability.
- **Example:** Marketers use phrases like "Only 3 left in stock" or "Limited-time offer" to drive immediate action. In social situations, appearing less available increases desirability.

By recognizing these predictable reactions, you can **subtly shape someone's decisions** without them realizing they are being influenced.

Behavioral Conditioning: The Key to Long-Term Control

Short-term manipulation is useful, but the real power lies in **long-term behavioral conditioning**. If you can shape a person's responses over time, they will unconsciously follow the patterns you set for them.

There are two key methods to achieve this:

Positive Reinforcement

This involves rewarding desired behavior to encourage repetition. The **reward doesn't have to be tangible**—praise, social approval, or emotional validation can be just as effective as money or gifts.

- **Example:** A manipulator gradually reinforces a specific behavior in a partner by reacting positively when they act in a way that aligns with the manipulator's goals.

Negative Conditioning

This involves discouraging unwanted behavior through subtle forms of disapproval, discomfort, or mild punishment. Unlike overt aggression, negative conditioning is **subtle and deniable**—making the target unaware they are being controlled.

- **Example:** If a manipulator wants to discourage independence in a friend or partner, they might withdraw affection or subtly guilt-trip them whenever they make decisions alone. Over time, the target learns to seek approval by aligning with the manipulator's desires.

Both techniques are most effective when applied **incrementally**. If changes happen too suddenly, the target may resist. But if they occur gradually, the person accepts them as normal behavior.

How to Use Predictability to Influence Others

The final step in leveraging behavioral predictability is **positioning yourself as a guiding force** in a person's decision-making process.

Here's how to do it:

1. **Observe:** Watch for patterns in how a person responds to different situations. Identify their emotional triggers, habits, and decision-making tendencies.
2. **Anticipate:** Based on their past behavior, predict how they will react in similar situations.
3. **Subtly steer:** Present choices in a way that aligns with their natural inclinations while guiding them toward your desired outcome.
4. **Reinforce:** Use positive or negative reinforcement to strengthen the behaviors you want.
5. **Gradually escalate:** Once they accept small changes, introduce larger ones, ensuring compliance at each step.

By recognizing that **people are not as independent as they believe**, you can craft interactions that lead them exactly where you want them to go. True manipulation is not about forcing actions—it is about **creating conditions where the target willingly follows the path you set for them**.

Subtlety Wins: Why Obvious Manipulation Fails

The most effective manipulation is the kind that goes unnoticed. When people feel they are being controlled, they resist. This is why direct coercion often backfires—it triggers **psychological reactance**, a defensive response that makes individuals push back against perceived threats to their autonomy.

Skilled manipulators understand that the key to influence is **subtlety**. The best manipulation techniques are those that feel natural to the target. When someone believes they are acting of their own free will, they are far more likely to comply with the desired outcome.

In this chapter, we will explore why obvious manipulation fails, how people detect influence attempts, and the techniques used to ensure manipulation remains hidden.

Why People Resist Direct Control

Humans have an instinctual desire for autonomy. This is rooted in **self-determination theory**, which suggests that people are motivated by three core psychological needs:

1. **Autonomy:** The feeling of being in control of one's own actions.
2. **Competence:** The desire to feel capable and effective.
3. **Relatedness:** The need for connection and belonging.

When someone realizes they are being manipulated, their **autonomy is threatened**. The natural response is to resist, even if the influence is in their best interest.

The Psychological Reactance Effect

Psychological reactance occurs when people perceive an attempt to limit their freedom. Instead of complying, they often do the opposite just to reassert control.

- ▶ **Example:** A teenager explicitly told not to date someone may become even more determined to pursue the relationship.
- ▶ **Example:** A customer pressured by an aggressive salesperson is more likely to walk away than make a purchase.

This resistance isn't logical—it's emotional. The mere act of **recognizing** an influence attempt triggers an automatic rejection response.

The solution? **Ensure that the target never realizes they are being manipulated.**

How People Detect Manipulation

People are naturally suspicious of influence tactics, especially when they feel unnatural or forced. Here are the key red flags that make manipulation obvious:

1. Overt Pressure

Any attempt to force an outcome makes people defensive. When someone senses urgency or desperation in an influencer's behavior, they instinctively resist.

- **Example:** A boss who constantly tells employees, *"You must do this exactly as I say,"* breeds resentment.
- **Example:** A date who says, *"If you really cared about me, you'd do this,"* triggers alarm bells.

Subtle alternative: Instead of direct pressure, use **implied expectations**—people comply more readily when they believe it was their own choice.

2. Excessive Compliments or Flattery

Flattery can be effective, but when it feels excessive or insincere, it raises suspicion.

- **Example:** A stranger who immediately showers someone with praise often comes across as manipulative rather than genuine.
- **Example:** A salesperson who constantly compliments a customer's taste may seem inauthentic.

Subtle alternative: Instead of over-the-top flattery, use **calibrated validation**—compliments that feel earned and specific rather than general and excessive.

3. Logical Inconsistencies

People detect manipulation when they notice contradictions in someone's behavior or arguments.

- **Example:** A boss who says *"We're a team,"* but constantly takes credit for others' work erodes trust.
- **Example:** A political leader who claims to support transparency while hiding critical information creates doubt.

Subtle alternative: Ensure consistency in words and actions. If deception is necessary, maintain a logical framework that cannot be easily questioned.

4. Overuse of Guilt or Fear

Manipulators who rely too heavily on guilt or fear often trigger resentment. If someone feels emotionally blackmailed, they will resist compliance.

- **Example:** A partner who constantly says, *"If you loved me, you'd do this,"* fosters emotional exhaustion.
- **Example:** A leader who governs through fear will eventually lose influence when people become desensitized.

Subtle alternative: Use **social proof and consensus** instead of direct emotional pressure. People are more likely to conform if they believe others already have.

How to Make Manipulation Invisible

The best manipulation feels organic. Here are the techniques that keep influence hidden while ensuring compliance.

1. The Illusion of Choice

People comply more readily when they believe they are making a choice—even if both options lead to the same desired outcome.

- **Example:** Instead of saying, *"Sign this contract,"* a skilled negotiator asks, *"Would you prefer to sign today or tomorrow?"*
- **Example:** Instead of forcing a friend to go out, say, *"Should we go to the club or the lounge?"*—both options accomplish the goal of going out.

By presenting **controlled options**, the influencer allows the target to feel autonomous while still directing their decision.

2. The Power of Suggestion

Direct commands often trigger resistance. Instead, the best manipulators **plant ideas subtly**, allowing the target to come to conclusions on their own.

- **Example:** Instead of saying, *"You should trust me,"* a skilled manipulator says, *"You're someone who values loyalty, right?"*—which leads the target toward trust naturally.
- **Example:** Instead of saying, *"You need to invest in this,"* a financial advisor might say, *"Smart investors are looking at this opportunity right now."*

This technique shifts the target's perception without making them feel coerced.

3. Leading with Small Agreements

People are more likely to comply with a larger request if they first agree to a smaller one.

- **Example:** A political activist first asks people to sign a petition (a minor commitment). Later, they ask them to donate money—the prior agreement increases the likelihood of compliance.
- **Example:** A date who first gets someone to agree to a small outing (coffee) can more easily escalate to a bigger date (dinner).

Each small agreement reinforces a psychological pattern that makes further compliance feel natural.

4. The Role of Time and Patience

True manipulation is **gradual**. Sudden attempts to control someone often fail because they feel unnatural. However, when influence happens slowly over time, the target **fails to recognize the shift**.

- **Example:** A cult doesn't immediately demand extreme loyalty—it starts with small commitments, escalating them over weeks or months.

- **Example:** A boss who wants an employee to take on more responsibilities first asks for minor tasks, slowly increasing expectations until the employee accepts a much larger workload without protest.

Incremental influence creates **habitual compliance**, ensuring that manipulation remains unnoticed.

The Golden Rule: Make It Feel Natural

The fundamental principle behind subtle manipulation is **blending into the target's reality**. If influence feels out of place or forced, it will be resisted. However, if it aligns with the target's existing beliefs, emotions, and habits, it will be accepted.

To ensure manipulation remains undetected:

- **Avoid direct pressure:** Guide, don't force.
- **Let the target believe it was their idea:** Use suggestion instead of commands.
- **Control the choices available:** Never present a true "no" option.
- **Make changes gradual:** Sudden shifts trigger resistance; slow influence is unnoticed.
- **Remain consistent:** Contradictions create suspicion.

By mastering the art of subtlety, manipulation becomes seamless. The most successful influencers are those who never seem like they are influencing at all.

Control the Frame, Control the Outcome

Every interaction takes place within a **frame**—a mental lens through which people interpret reality. The frame dictates what is important, how events should be understood, and what conclusions should be drawn. Whoever controls the frame controls the conversation, the perception of truth, and ultimately, the outcome.

The power of framing is used in business, politics, media, and interpersonal relationships to manipulate thought and behavior. Understanding how to establish, maintain, and shift frames is a crucial skill for anyone seeking to influence others without direct force.

What is Framing?

Framing is the act of defining how a situation is perceived. It determines **context, emotional tone, and meaning** before a discussion even begins. The frame tells people **what matters and what doesn't.**

Consider a simple example:

- *Frame 1:* "This surgery has a 90% success rate." (Optimistic perspective)
- *Frame 2:* "This surgery has a 10% failure rate." (Pessimistic perspective)

Both statements contain identical information, but they trigger different emotional responses. People are more likely to accept the first frame, even though the facts haven't changed.

Now apply this concept to real-world scenarios:

- **Politics:** A new law can be framed as "enhancing national security" or "reducing personal freedoms" depending on who presents it.
- **Business:** A failing company can be framed as "undergoing a necessary restructuring" rather than "collapsing under financial pressure."
- **Social Influence:** A manipulator can frame their excessive control as "being protective" rather than "being controlling."

Key Principle: The person who defines the frame defines reality.

If you fail to set the frame, someone else will set it for you. And once a frame is established, it is incredibly difficult to break.

The Power of Pre-Framing

Pre-framing is the act of **setting expectations before** a conversation or event takes place. It ensures that the target enters the situation already primed to see things from a specific angle.

Example 1: Sales & Business

Imagine a salesperson introducing a product:

- **Without pre-framing:** *"This is a new product on the market."*

- **With pre-framing:** *"This product is being used by top executives to boost productivity."*

The second version **pre-frames** the product as something exclusive and desirable before the details are even discussed.

Example 2: Social Dynamics
A manipulator in a relationship might pre-frame their actions:

- *"I just care about you so much, I want to be involved in every part of your life."*

By framing **control** as **care**, they reduce resistance before the target even questions their behavior.

How to Use Pre-Framing:
1. **Define the narrative before others do.**
2. **Use language that shapes perception.**
3. **Ensure the first impression aligns with your desired outcome.**

Reframing: Shifting Perception Mid-Conversation

If someone else sets a frame that does not work in your favor, you must **reframe** the situation. Reframing changes how the same information is perceived, altering emotional responses and decisions.

Example: Handling Accusations
Imagine someone accuses you of being "too aggressive" in a negotiation. Instead of defending yourself, you **reframe**:

- *"I'm not aggressive, I'm just highly focused on getting the best outcome for everyone involved."*

Now, instead of seeming combative, you appear **goal-oriented** and **strategic**. The original accusation loses power.

Example: Turning Weakness into Strength
If someone says, "You're inexperienced in this field," you can reframe:

- *"That's exactly why I bring a fresh perspective that others don't have."*

This turns a perceived weakness into an advantage, altering how others see you.

How to Use Reframing:

- **Listen for negative frames.** Identify when someone else is shaping perception against your interests.
- **Immediately reframe using different language.**
- **Shift the focus toward an advantage.**

Controlling Emotional Frames

Framing doesn't just apply to facts—it also dictates emotions. If you control the **emotional frame** of a conversation, you control how people feel about a situation.

1. The Power of Calmness

People mirror the emotions of those around them. If you remain calm in a heated situation, others will subconsciously follow your lead.

- **Example:** If someone is angry at you, responding with absolute calmness forces them to reconsider their emotional reaction.

2. Creating a Sense of Urgency

Urgency increases compliance. When people believe time is limited, they are more likely to act without thinking critically.

- **Example:** Marketers create urgency with phrases like *"Limited time offer"* or *"Only a few spots left."*

3. The Authority Frame

Authority frames make people **default to compliance**. When an idea is framed as coming from a trusted expert, it is far more persuasive.

- **Example:** Instead of saying, "I think this is a good investment," say, "Top financial analysts agree this is a strong investment opportunity."

By controlling the **emotional** tone of a situation, you shape **how** people respond—without them realizing why.

Frame Stacking: Controlling Conversations from Start to Finish

The most powerful manipulators don't just use one frame—they stack multiple frames together to create a **layered reality** that supports their goal.

Example: Selling a Luxury Service

A high-end consultant might **stack frames** like this:

1. **Pre-Frame:** "The most successful business leaders understand the power of investing in elite guidance." (This sets an expectation that elite professionals invest in coaching.)
2. **Emotional Frame:** "Think about how much faster you'll reach your goals with an expert guiding you." (Creates excitement and FOMO.)
3. **Authority Frame:** "This method has been used by Fortune 500 CEOs." (Adds credibility.)
4. **Scarcity Frame:** "I only take on a few clients per year." (Creates urgency.)
5. **Social Proof Frame:** "90% of my clients see major improvements in their businesses within three months." (Adds reassurance.)

By stacking multiple frames, the target is surrounded by a reality that **makes compliance feel inevitable**.

Defensive Strategies: Breaking Free from Framing Manipulation

If someone else is controlling the frame, you must break out of it to **regain control** over your own perception. Here's how:

1. Question the Premise

If someone presents a frame you don't agree with, don't argue within their frame—challenge its foundation.

- **Manipulative Frame:** *"Since you don't care about the team, you must not want to participate."*
- **Breaking It:** *"Who said I don't care about the team? I actually want what's best for everyone, which is why I have concerns."*

2. Introduce a Counter-Frame

If someone sets a negative frame, immediately establish a competing one.

- **Manipulative Frame:** *"This deal is your only real option."*
- **Counter-Frame:** *"Actually, I'm considering multiple options and looking for the best fit."*

3. Control Emotional Tone

Don't let someone else's emotions dictate the interaction. Stay composed, neutral, and assertive.

By recognizing and dismantling manipulative frames, you take back control over how you interpret and respond to situations.

Final Thoughts: Control the Frame, Control the World

Framing is the invisible force that shapes perception. Those who understand it **dictate reality** for others, making them incredibly powerful in business, politics, relationships, and social dynamics.

To master framing:

1. **Always pre-frame situations to your advantage.**
2. **Use reframing to shift perception in your favor.**
3. **Stack multiple frames for maximum influence.**
4. **Recognize and resist negative framing attempts.**

The person who controls the frame **controls the outcome**—and most people never realize it's happening.

CHAPTER 2

THE SCIENCE OF SUGGESTION – HOW TO IMPLANT IDEAS

The ability to implant ideas into someone's mind without them realizing it is one of the most powerful tools of manipulation. Unlike overt persuasion, which invites scrutiny and resistance, suggestion works subtly, slipping thoughts into the subconscious where they feel like the target's own ideas.

This chapter explores the mechanisms behind subconscious influence, revealing how thoughts can be planted, reinforced, and shaped to guide decision-making without direct coercion. By mastering these techniques, you will be able to manipulate perception effortlessly—whether in business, relationships, or everyday interactions.

The Subconscious Planting Method

The subconscious mind is the true decision-maker. While people believe they act based on logical reasoning, neuroscience shows that most decisions are made **before** conscious awareness catches up. The subconscious processes **associations, emotions, and past experiences**, shaping beliefs and guiding actions.

By subtly influencing this hidden decision-making system, you can plant ideas in someone's mind in a way that feels completely natural. The key is to bypass their **critical thinking filters** and embed suggestions deep enough that they take root.

How the Subconscious Accepts Ideas

The subconscious is **highly receptive** to certain types of input. To successfully implant an idea, you must follow a psychological process that aligns with how the brain naturally absorbs information.

1. Lowering Mental Defenses

A person's conscious mind acts as a **gatekeeper**, filtering out ideas that seem suspicious, contradictory, or forced. The first step to planting a thought is to **reduce mental resistance** so that the subconscious becomes more open to influence.

How to do it:

- **Use Relaxation:** People are more suggestible when they are calm, distracted, or in a passive state (e.g., watching TV, engaging in small talk, or listening to music).
- **Build Rapport:** When someone feels connected to you, they are less likely to question your words critically.
- **Use Indirect Communication:** Avoid direct commands or arguments—suggestions are more effective when they don't seem like persuasion.

Example: Instead of saying, *"You should trust me,"* say, *"You know, it's interesting how some people naturally build trust with others."*

This indirect phrasing **lowers defenses** while subtly leading the person toward trust.

2. Using Emotional Associations

The subconscious doesn't process ideas through logic—it responds to **feelings, patterns, and associations**. If an idea is linked to a strong emotional response, it becomes deeply embedded in memory.

How to do it:

- **Pair the Idea with an Emotion:** Frame your suggestion in a way that triggers excitement, nostalgia, fear, or desire.
- **Use Personal Triggers:** Reference something meaningful to the target (a shared experience, a personal value, or a strong belief).
- **Anchor the Emotion to a Repeated Stimulus:** Repeatedly associate an idea with a specific emotional state to reinforce it.

Example: If you want someone to feel attached to you, repeatedly **associate your presence with positive emotions**—laughter, comfort, shared success.

Over time, their brain will link **you** with **happiness**, making them more likely to trust and follow your lead.

3. Embedding the Idea Subconsciously

Once the mind is primed, the next step is to introduce the idea in a way that feels organic. The goal is for the target to **internalize the thought as their own**.

How to do it:

- **Use Stories & Metaphors:** The brain is wired to absorb stories more easily than direct statements. A well-crafted anecdote can carry a hidden suggestion without triggering resistance.
- **Implant the Thought Indirectly:** Instead of telling someone what to think, let them reach the conclusion themselves through guided questions.
- **Use Social Proof:** People trust ideas more when they believe others already accept them. Frame the idea as something that "most smart people already believe."

Example: Instead of saying, *"You should quit your job and start a business,"* say, *"It's interesting how many people are realizing that working for themselves gives them more freedom."*

This shifts the **burden of decision-making** onto the target, making the thought feel like something **they** arrived at naturally.

Case Study: The Power of Indirect Influence

Consider how **advertisers manipulate perception** without direct persuasion. Instead of saying, *"Buy our product,"* they use:

- **Subtle Placement:** Showing the product in the hands of celebrities or in an aspirational lifestyle setting.
- **Emotional Hooks:** Associating the brand with happiness, success, or exclusivity.
- **Repetition & Familiarity:** The more often you see a brand, the more you subconsciously trust it.

The **same techniques** apply in social and professional interactions. If you want someone to see you as **a leader**, don't tell them outright—instead, surround yourself with people who already treat you as one, and let **subconscious association** do the work.

How to Make the Thought Stick

The final step in subconscious implantation is **reinforcement**. A single suggestion is often forgotten, but repeated exposure **solidifies the idea**.

1. Repeat Subtly, Not Forcefully

The brain rejects overt repetition, but **subtle exposure over time** creates familiarity and acceptance.

- **Example:** If you want a colleague to support your idea, mention it casually in different conversations **without pushing too hard**.

2. Get the Target to Say It Themselves

People believe ideas **more strongly when they say them out loud**. Encourage the target to **verbalize** your suggestion in their own words.

- **Example:** Instead of saying, *"You should take this job,"* say, *"What do you think are the biggest benefits of this job for you?"*
- Once they list the positives themselves, their brain takes ownership of the idea.

3. Use Environmental Triggers

Link the idea to **external cues** that repeatedly reinforce it.

- **Example:** If you want someone to associate you with ambition, **place symbols of success** (books, awards, luxury items) in your space when they visit.
- The subconscious **absorbs** the message without a word being spoken.

Application: Using the Subconscious Planting Method in Daily Life

This technique can be applied in **business, relationships, and social influence:**

- ▸ **In Business:** Want a client to see you as the best choice? Subtly frame your expertise through **stories**, encourage them to **voice their own reasoning**, and reinforce the perception through social proof.
- ▸ **In Dating & Relationships:** Want someone to feel a deep emotional connection? **Associate yourself with their happiest moments**, implant thoughts through indirect suggestion, and let them **verbalize their feelings first**.
- ▸ **In Leadership & Negotiation:** Want to guide a decision? **Shape expectations subtly**, introduce your suggestion **indirectly**, and let repetition reinforce the idea until it becomes reality.

By **bypassing the conscious mind** and working through the **subconscious**, you create influence that is **far more powerful than direct persuasion**.

Final Thought: The Art of Invisible Influence

When done correctly, **subconscious planting feels natural to the target**. They will believe they arrived at the thought on their own, making them far more likely to act on it. The key is to remain **subtle, patient, and strategic**.

To master this technique:

1. **Lower resistance** by keeping communication indirect.
2. **Attach emotions** to reinforce the idea.
3. **Encourage self-verbalization** for ownership.
4. **Use repetition and environment** for reinforcement.

A well-planted idea can **change behavior permanently**—without the target ever realizing how it happened.

Indirect Influence: Making People Think It Was Their Idea

The most powerful form of manipulation is when the target believes they arrived at a conclusion **on their own**. When people feel they are making an independent choice, they embrace it more fully and resist it less. This is why **indirect influence** is far superior to direct persuasion.

Instead of telling someone what to do, a skilled manipulator **guides them subtly** toward the desired outcome—without them realizing they are being led. This technique is used in **sales, leadership, negotiations, relationships, and even politics** to shape decisions while maintaining the illusion of autonomy.

In this section, we will explore **how to steer people's thinking** so that your desired idea feels like **theirs**—making compliance effortless.

Why Direct Persuasion Fails

Traditional persuasion often involves **arguing, convincing, or pressuring** someone into agreement. The problem? Direct persuasion **triggers resistance**.

Psychological Reactance: The Rebellion Effect

Humans have an instinctive desire for **autonomy**. When they sense an attempt to control their thinking, they push back—even if the argument is logical. This reaction is known as **psychological reactance**.

- **Example 1:** A teenager is told *"You're not allowed to see that person."* Instead of compliance, this restriction **increases** their desire to see that person.
- **Example 2:** A customer is told, *"This is the best deal you'll find anywhere."* They immediately **doubt** the claim and look for alternatives.

The solution? **Never tell someone directly what to do.** Instead, create an environment where they **arrive at your desired conclusion on their own.**

The Art of Indirect Influence

To make someone believe an idea is theirs, use the following techniques:

1. Guided Questions: Leading Without Telling

Instead of telling someone what to think, **ask questions that guide them toward the answer you want**. This technique is commonly used in sales, therapy, and leadership.

- **Direct persuasion (bad approach):** *"You should buy this because it's the best option."*
- **Indirect influence (better approach):** *"What's most important to you in a product like this?"*

By asking questions, you make the target actively engage in **justifying the decision for themselves**.

Examples in Action:

- **Negotiation:** *"How do you see this benefiting you in the long run?"*
- **Leadership:** *"What do you think would happen if we tried this new approach?"*
- **Sales:** *"What's the biggest frustration with your current solution?"*

Once they verbalize the **answer you want**, they feel **psychological ownership** over the decision.

2. The Illusion of Choice: Controlling the Options

People resist commands, but they like **making choices**. The trick is to **control the available choices** so that **all paths lead to your desired outcome**.

- **Bad approach:** *"You need to sign this contract."*
- **Better approach:** *"Would you prefer to start the project this week or next week?"*

By offering two choices, both of which align with your goal, you create **an illusion of control** while still guiding the decision.

Examples in Action:

- **Parenting:** *"Do you want to do your homework before or after dinner?"* (Either way, the homework gets done.)
- **Management:** *"Would you rather lead the new project or collaborate on it?"* (Either way, they take responsibility.)
- **Dating:** *"Do you want to grab drinks or check out that new restaurant?"* (Either way, they agree to go out.)

The **illusion of choice** makes compliance **feel voluntary**, reducing resistance.

3. Social Proof: The Power of Group Influence

People naturally conform to **what others are doing**. Instead of telling someone what to do, frame it as **something many others are already doing.**

- **Bad approach:** *"You should try this."*
- **Better approach:** *"Most people in your situation go with this option."*

By positioning an idea as the norm, people accept it without questioning it.

Examples in Action:

- **Sales:** *"90% of customers choose this plan."*
- **Workplace Influence:** *"Most top employees use this strategy to stay productive."*
- **Relationships:** *"Everyone I know who tried this said it changed their perspective."*

People are less likely to **resist an idea** if they believe it's already **widely accepted**.

4. Priming: Influencing Thoughts Before They Happen

Priming involves subtly exposing someone to **specific ideas, words, or emotions** before a decision, making them more likely to think in a certain way **without realizing why**.

- **Example 1:** A waiter **mentions desserts** at the start of a meal. When the check arrives, customers are **more likely to order dessert** because the idea was implanted earlier.

- **Example 2:** A recruiter **praises a candidate's leadership skills** before discussing a management role. The candidate **starts seeing themselves as a leader** before the job is even offered.

How to Use Priming:

- **Use specific words in conversation that subtly reinforce your idea.**
    - (e.g., Repeatedly saying "trust" makes someone subconsciously associate you with trustworthiness.)
- **Expose people to concepts before making a request.**
    - (e.g., Talking about "success" before negotiating a raise makes success feel more achievable.)
- **Set a positive emotional tone before persuasion.**
    - (e.g., Making someone laugh before making a request makes them more receptive.)

Priming **bypasses logical resistance** by shaping perception **before** a decision is made.

Real-World Applications of Indirect Influence

1. Sales & Business

Want to close a deal? Instead of pushing a sale, **ask guided questions**, use **social proof**, and frame the purchase as **a natural choice**.

- *"Most successful professionals invest in this kind of training. What's most important for you in growing your career?"*

Now, the buyer feels like they made the choice themselves.

2. Leadership & Negotiation

Want employees or partners to follow your vision? **Let them believe it was their idea.**

- *"How do you think we can improve efficiency?"*
- When they suggest **your desired solution**, they take **ownership of the idea** and support it more strongly.

3. Dating & Relationships

Want someone to feel closer to you? **Subtly reinforce emotions** before they recognize them.

- *"Isn't it amazing how some connections just feel effortless?"*
- This plants the idea that **your relationship feels effortless**, influencing how they perceive it.

How to Make Indirect Influence Stick

For maximum effectiveness, combine multiple techniques:

- **Ask guided questions** to lead their thinking.
- **Create the illusion of choice** to reduce resistance.
- **Use social proof** to make the decision feel normal.
- **Prime their mind** before presenting an idea.

When done correctly, the target will **not only accept your idea**—they will believe it was theirs from the start.

Final Thought: The Power of Letting People Convince Themselves

People trust their own conclusions more than anything they are told. The best manipulators understand this and use **subtle techniques to plant thoughts, steer perception, and create buy-in—without ever appearing to influence at all.**

Mastering indirect influence allows you to **shape reality** while making the target **feel in complete control**.

Repetition & Priming: The Psychological Trojan Horse

Repetition and priming are two of the most powerful tools for embedding thoughts into the subconscious mind. Unlike direct persuasion, which triggers resistance, these methods **bypass critical thinking** and make ideas feel natural, familiar, and self-generated.

Repetition ensures an idea **sticks**, while priming prepares the brain **to accept it** before the target even realizes they are being influenced. Advertisers, politicians, and manipulators use these techniques daily to shape perceptions, decisions, and behaviors without direct coercion.

Understanding how to use repetition and priming allows you to implant ideas that people will believe **simply because they've heard them enough times.**

The Science of Repetition: Why Familiarity Feels Like Truth

The **illusory truth effect** is a psychological phenomenon in which people start believing **false** information if they hear it repeatedly. This is because the brain associates **familiarity with accuracy.**

A 1977 study by Hasher, Goldstein, and Toppino demonstrated this effect: participants were more likely to believe a statement was true after encountering it multiple times—even when it was completely false.

This explains why:

- Advertisers repeat slogans until they become ingrained in memory.
- Political figures repeat talking points to reinforce public belief.
- Myths and rumors persist despite being debunked.

Example: If you repeatedly hear, *"You need eight glasses of water a day,"* you are likely to believe it—even though no scientific study supports this claim.

Repetition works because **the brain takes shortcuts**—instead of analyzing every statement critically, it assumes that if something sounds familiar, it must be true.

How to Use Repetition to Implant Ideas

1. Repeat Key Messages in Different Ways

Saying the **same thing the same way** over and over can seem unnatural or forceful. Instead, **restate the same idea in varied forms** to reinforce it without triggering resistance.

- **Example (Sales):** Instead of saying, *"This product is the best,"* repeatedly, frame it in different ways:

- *"A lot of people are saying this is the best option."*
- *"This product consistently outperforms others in its category."*
- *"The results speak for themselves—this product dominates the market."*

By varying phrasing, you increase exposure **without seeming repetitive**.

2. Create "Echo Chambers" of Information

People are more likely to believe something if they **hear it from multiple sources.**

- **Example (Social Influence):** A manipulator who wants to convince a target that a person is untrustworthy will ensure they hear this message from **multiple people**:

- *"I've heard John isn't reliable."*
- *"Did you know John has let people down in the past?"*
- *"You might want to be careful with John."*

By engineering **multiple points of reinforcement**, the target will start to accept the idea **as their own belief**.

3. Subtly Reinforce Through Casual Conversation

Repetition does not always have to be obvious. The best manipulators embed their key messages in **normal conversations** over time.

- **Example (Relationships):** Instead of saying, *"You should trust me,"* repeatedly, a skilled manipulator might say:

- *"It's rare to find someone you can really trust."*
- *"I've always valued honesty in relationships."*
- *"Trust is the foundation of everything."*

The more the idea is introduced, the **deeper it takes root** in the target's subconscious.

Priming: Influencing Thoughts Before They Happen

While repetition reinforces beliefs, **priming sets the stage for those beliefs to form in the first place**. Priming works by **exposing the subconscious to certain words, images, or ideas** before a decision or action takes place, making those ideas more accessible in the mind.

A famous study by Bargh, Chen, and Burrows (1996) demonstrated this effect: participants who were subtly exposed to **words related to aging** (like "slow," "forgetful," and "gray") **walked more slowly afterward**, even though they were unaware of the connection.

This shows that **the subconscious absorbs influences** without conscious awareness, leading to **predictable behavioral changes**.

How to Use Priming to Influence Decisions

1. Use Language to Set Expectations

Words **shape perception** before a person even thinks about a situation. By strategically choosing certain words or phrases, you influence how someone **interprets events**.

- **Example (Leadership):** Instead of saying, *"We have a tough challenge ahead,"* say, *"We have a great opportunity to grow."*
- **Example (Sales):** Instead of saying, *"This is a cheap product,"* say, *"This is a high-value investment."*

Priming **sets the mental tone** for how information is received.

2. Introduce Ideas Indirectly Before Presenting a Request

If you want someone to agree with you, **introduce the concept subtly before making the direct request.**

- **Example (Negotiation):**
    - **Before proposing a salary increase**, casually mention industry standards for competitive wages in an unrelated conversation.
    - Later, when you bring up your request, the target's mind is already **primed** to view higher salaries as reasonable.

By **laying the groundwork,** your suggestion **feels logical and expected.**

3. Use Environmental Cues to Shape Mood and Perception

Priming doesn't just work through words—it also works through **physical and sensory cues**.

- **Example (Business Deals):** Meetings held in **large rooms with high ceilings** make people feel **more open-minded, leading to greater willingness to consider new ideas.**
- **Example (Sales Psychology)**: Restaurants use **soft lighting** and **slow music** to prime customers to relax and stay longer, increasing spending.

Manipulating an environment manipulates the thoughts and emotions within it.

Combining Repetition and Priming for Maximum Influence

While each method is powerful on its own, the **greatest impact** comes from **combining repetition and priming** to shape a person's thoughts from multiple angles.

Example: Creating Brand Loyalty

A company wants customers to associate their brand with **luxury and exclusivity**. They use:

1. **Priming** – The brand uses **high-status imagery** (celebrities, sleek designs) to **prepare the audience's mind** before they even consider purchasing.
2. **Repetition** – The message is reinforced in **advertisements, social media, and word-of-mouth recommendations**.
3. **Environmental Influence** – When customers enter the store, **the lighting, music, and scent all match the "luxury" feeling**, further reinforcing the association.

By the time the customer makes a decision, **they already believe in the brand's exclusivity**—without even knowing why.

Using These Techniques in Daily Life

- **In Sales & Business:** Repeat key benefits in different ways, **prime expectations before negotiations**, and use multiple sources for reinforcement.
- **In Relationships:** Prime people to see you **as trustworthy, valuable, or exciting** by subtly reinforcing these traits over time.
- **In Leadership:** Set the frame early, repeat key messages, and **use environmental priming** to shape behavior.

Final Thought: Why People Never Realize They've Been Influenced

The power of **repetition and priming** lies in their **invisibility**. People never stop to question **why** they believe something if the thought **feels familiar** or **seems natural**.

Mastering these techniques allows you to:

1. **Plant ideas subtly.**
2. **Make concepts feel familiar and true.**
3. **Influence decisions before they happen.**

When done correctly, the target **will believe they arrived at the thought themselves**—making them far more likely to act on it.

The Zeigarnik Effect: How Unfinished Thoughts Create Obsession

One of the most powerful psychological tools in manipulation is **the Zeigarnik Effect**—a cognitive phenomenon where the brain **fixates on unfinished tasks and unresolved thoughts**. This effect can be used to create **mental loops, emotional intrigue, and a deep sense of urgency**, making people unable to stop thinking about an idea, a person, or a situation.

Advertisers, writers, salespeople, and even seducers use this technique to **leave thoughts open-ended**, ensuring that their target remains engaged long after the interaction is over.

This section explores how to use the Zeigarnik Effect to keep people's minds occupied with **your** desired thoughts—whether in business, relationships, or persuasion.

What is the Zeigarnik Effect?

The **Zeigarnik Effect** was first identified in the 1920s by Soviet psychologist **Bluma Zeigarnik**, who noticed that waiters in a restaurant could **remember unpaid orders with great detail** but quickly forgot them after the bill was settled.

Her experiments confirmed that **people remember and dwell on unfinished tasks far more than completed ones.** The brain naturally seeks **closure**, and when something is left unresolved, it creates **mental tension** that keeps the idea active in the subconscious.

This is why:

- **Cliffhanger endings make people desperate for the next episode.**
- **Unanswered questions linger in the mind longer than complete answers.**
- **When someone stops mid-story, we feel compelled to ask, "What happened next?"**

When used intentionally, this effect **creates intrigue, increases engagement, and makes ideas unforgettable.**

How to Use the Zeigarnik Effect for Influence

1. Create Open Loops in Conversation

People **hate** unfinished thoughts. When a story, question, or idea is left incomplete, the mind naturally **tries to close the loop**—even long after the conversation ends.

- **Example (Business & Sales):**
    - Instead of saying, *"Our product improves efficiency by 30%,"* say,
        - *"The way our product increases efficiency is really surprising... Let me explain."*
    - By introducing **a sense of mystery**, you keep the target **mentally engaged**, making them eager to learn more.

- **Example (Relationships & Social Influence):**
  - If you say, *"There's something interesting I noticed about you..."* but pause before explaining, the person will **fixate on what you were going to say** until they hear it.
  - Their brain **obsesses over filling the gap**, making them more invested in the interaction.

The more **unfinished loops** you create, the more **mentally occupied** your target becomes.

2. Use Cliffhangers to Maintain Interest

The entertainment industry **thrives** on the Zeigarnik Effect. Every great TV show, book, or movie uses **cliffhangers** to ensure audiences return.

- **Example (Marketing):**
  - "We're about to release something groundbreaking... stay tuned."
  - This **keeps people engaged** and eager for the next update.

- **Example (Dating & Personal Influence):**
  - Instead of answering a question directly, say:
    - *"That's a crazy story... but I'll tell you later."*
  - This **creates anticipation**, ensuring the person keeps thinking about you.

By delaying closure, you increase curiosity, emotional investment, and attachment.

3. Interrupt Patterns to Leave a Lasting Impression

People expect **complete thoughts** in conversations. When you **intentionally disrupt** this pattern, it forces the brain to **hold onto the unfinished idea**.

- **Example (Sales & Business):**
  - Instead of making a full pitch, **pause strategically**:
    - *"The real reason this method works is..."* (pause) *"actually pretty fascinating."*
  - The **pause builds suspense**, making the listener lean in, hungry for the answer.

- **Example (Seduction & Influence):**
  - *"There's something I find incredibly attractive about you..."* (pause)
  - Leaving **a gap before finishing** forces the person's mind to **search for an answer**, making them more emotionally engaged.

By **breaking conversational flow at the right moment,** you make your words more **memorable and psychologically sticky.**

4. Use Unfinished Tasks to Keep People Hooked

People struggle to ignore **unfinished tasks**. You can use this to create a sense of **urgency and commitment**, making people feel compelled to **follow through**.

- **Example (Business & Marketing):**
  - Free trials exploit this principle by giving users **partial access** to a product. Once people start using something, they feel the need to **complete the experience** by purchasing the full version.
  - *"You're almost done—just one more step to unlock everything."*

- **Example (Relationships & Social Influence):**
  - If you text someone, *"I have something interesting to tell you..."* but don't follow up immediately, their brain **fixates on the unresolved statement**.
  - This increases **mental engagement and emotional investment**.

By **creating unfinished commitments,** you make people feel psychologically **compelled to take action.**

5. Make People Feel They Need to "Earn" Completion

The mind values **effort and investment**. If someone starts something but doesn't finish it, they feel a **need to complete the cycle**—even if they weren't fully committed before.

- **Example (Sales & Negotiation):**
  - Instead of offering everything upfront, make prospects **invest time before closing the deal**:

- *"I'll walk you through the first few steps, and if it makes sense, we'll take the next step."*
  - Once the prospect starts engaging, they feel internally driven to continue.

- **Example (Psychological Manipulation):**
  - If you want someone to **work harder for your attention**, reward them in **small increments** but never give them full validation immediately.
    - *"I really enjoy our conversations. But there's something I haven't quite figured out about you yet..."*
  - This creates **mystery and desire**, making them more eager to prove themselves.

People **hate leaving things unfinished**—the more you leverage this, the more you can control their **actions and emotional investment.**

How to Make the Zeigarnik Effect Work for You

To effectively use **unfinished thoughts to create obsession**, follow these principles:

1. **Leave conversations open-ended.** Never give **full closure** right away—create lingering curiosity.
2. **Use cliffhangers strategically.** Whether in marketing, storytelling, or relationships, leave **unfinished loops** that demand resolution.
3. **Make people invest before revealing everything.** The more effort they put in, the more **mentally engaged they become**.
4. **Break conversational patterns.** Introduce pauses, interruptions, or unexpected gaps to make statements **more memorable**.
5. **Use unresolved commitments to increase compliance.** Once someone starts something, they will **feel compelled to finish it**.

Final Thought: The Mind Cannot Ignore an Open Loop

The Zeigarnik Effect works because the brain seeks closure. If you master the ability to create unfinished thoughts, unanswered questions, and unresolved commitments, you can:

- **Make people think about you constantly.**
- **Create urgency and action where none existed.**
- **Ensure your ideas remain unforgettable.**

When done correctly, **the target will feel compelled to engage further**—without ever realizing they were manipulated.

CHAPTER 3
PSYCHOLOGICAL TRICKS FOR INFLUENCE

Influence is not about forcing people to comply—it's about making them **want** to follow your lead. The most skilled influencers use subtle psychological techniques that shape thoughts, decisions, and emotions without triggering resistance.

This chapter explores some of the most powerful psychological tricks for influence, including **mirroring, priming, anchoring, strategic silence, and the Yes-Ladder technique**. Each method works by **leveraging natural cognitive biases** to guide behavior while making the target believe they are acting of their own free will.

Mirroring: The Fastest Way to Build Trust

Mirroring is one of the most powerful psychological tricks for **building trust and influence quickly**. It is a natural, subconscious behavior where people **copy the body language, speech patterns, and emotions of those they feel connected to**.

By **intentionally** mirroring someone, you can **speed up trust-building**, create deeper rapport, and increase your ability to persuade without direct effort.

Why Mirroring Works: The Science of Rapport

Human beings are wired for **connection and social belonging**. When someone subtly mirrors our behavior, we subconsciously interpret it as a sign of similarity and **shared understanding**.

A 1999 study by Chartrand and Bargh demonstrated the power of mirroring. In their experiment, participants were **more likely to feel positively toward**

someone who mimicked their body language and speech patterns—even when they were unaware it was happening.

This effect occurs because **the brain associates similarity with safety and trust**. When people perceive someone as "like them," they are more likely to:

- Feel comfortable and at ease
- Be open to influence
- Trust the person without logical reasoning

This is why mirroring is **a common behavior in friendships, romantic relationships, and professional connections**.

Skilled influencers use mirroring **deliberately** to **accelerate trust and gain social advantage**.

How to Use Mirroring to Build Influence

1. Mirror Body Language Subtly

One of the easiest ways to build rapport is to **match the body language** of the person you are interacting with.

- If they **cross their arms**, wait a few seconds, then cross yours casually.
- If they **lean in**, subtly lean in as well.
- If they **gesture while speaking**, use similar hand movements.

The key is to make it **natural and unnoticeable. Overdoing it** makes mirroring feel **forced** and can backfire.

Example (Business): A negotiator subtly mirrors the posture of their counterpart, making the conversation feel **naturally comfortable and aligned**, increasing the likelihood of agreement.

2. Match Their Speaking Style and Tone

People feel more connected to those who **speak in a similar way**. Mirroring someone's speech patterns can **increase trust and likability almost instantly**.

Ways to mirror speech:

- Match **their pace**—if they speak quickly, slightly increase your speed; if they speak slowly, slow down.
- Use **similar phrases**—if they use casual language, avoid sounding overly formal.
- Adjust your **tone**—if they are calm and relaxed, soften your voice to match.

Example (Social Influence):

If someone says, *"I feel like this project is a huge challenge,"* instead of replying, *"No, it's easy,"* you could mirror their perspective:

- *"Yeah, I see what you mean. It does seem like a big challenge, but I think we can tackle it together."*

This subtle mirroring makes people feel **heard and understood**, increasing your ability to guide the conversation.

3. Reflect Their Emotional State

Mirroring is not just about body language and speech—it also applies to **emotions**. People naturally **trust and bond** with those who reflect their emotional experiences.

- If someone is **excited**, match their enthusiasm.
- If they are **frustrated**, acknowledge their feelings before steering toward a solution.

Example (Dating & Relationships):

- If someone says, *"I'm having such a stressful day,"* don't immediately try to fix it. Instead, **mirror their emotional state** first:
    - *"I hear you. That sounds exhausting."*
- Once they feel understood, they will be **far more receptive** to your influence.

4. Synchronize Actions to Build Deeper Rapport

Mirroring **works even when people are unaware it's happening**. One advanced technique is **synchronized movement**, where you subtly coordinate actions with someone in real time.

- If they **take a sip of their drink**, wait a few seconds and do the same.
- If they **adjust their posture**, shift slightly in response.
- If they **nod while speaking**, mirror it subtly.

This technique is especially powerful in **negotiations, sales, and social interactions**, as it creates a **non-verbal rhythm** that deepens connection.

Example (Negotiation):
A salesperson mirrors a potential buyer's relaxed posture and slow speech, **subtly reinforcing comfort and trust**, making the buyer more receptive to their offer.

How to Make Mirroring Feel Natural

Mirroring is only effective when **it goes unnoticed**. If the target **consciously recognizes** that they are being mirrored, the technique loses power.

To ensure natural execution:

- **Wait a few seconds before mirroring.** Sudden mirroring appears too obvious.
- **Be subtle.** Adjust posture, speech, and gestures **gradually**.
- **Don't overdo it.** If the target makes a sudden movement, don't instantly copy it—make mirroring feel **organic**.
- **Adapt based on the situation.** If someone is sad, don't **fully mirror their mood**—instead, show **understanding with a slightly uplifted tone** to lead them out of the emotion.

When done correctly, **mirroring makes the target feel deeply connected to you without understanding why.**

Advanced Mirroring: Leading the Interaction

Once rapport is established, a skilled manipulator can **reverse the mirroring effect** and subtly take control of the interaction.

Step 1: Mirror First to Build Trust

- Start by **matching their behavior** to create alignment.

Step 2: Gradually Change Your Behavior

- Slowly shift your **posture, tone, or gestures** to a different state.
- If they follow your shift **without realizing it**, you now control the dynamic.

Step 3: Use Leading Mirroring to Direct Outcomes

- If you want them to **be more confident**, subtly shift your own posture into a **more dominant position** and watch as they follow.
- If you want to **calm someone down**, **slow your speech** and **relax your breathing**—they will subconsciously mirror the change.

This technique is used in **leadership, negotiations, and social engineering** to guide behavior **without appearing forceful**.

Example (Business Leadership):

A CEO begins by mirroring an employee's concerned body language. Once trust is built, they **shift into a more confident posture**, leading the employee into a **state of reassurance and motivation**.

Final Thought: Why Mirroring is So Powerful

Mirroring is a **silent but powerful** technique that creates deep psychological bonds. When used effectively, it allows you to:

- **Establish trust quickly**
- **Increase likability and influence**
- **Subconsciously guide interactions**
- **Control the emotional tone of a conversation**

Most importantly, mirroring **makes people feel naturally drawn to you** without them ever realizing why.

Master this technique, and you will hold **instant influence over anyone you meet**.

The Illusion of Certainty: How Confidence Overrides Truth

Imagine two people presenting the same argument. One speaks with hesitation, carefully choosing their words, acknowledging uncertainties. The other delivers the same information with absolute certainty, unwavering eye contact, and a firm voice. **Who do you believe?**

For most people, the answer is the second speaker. Not because their argument is stronger, but because their **confidence makes it feel more true**. This is the **Illusion of Certainty**—the psychological bias that makes people equate **certainty with correctness**.

From **sales and politics to personal relationships**, those who master **the appearance of certainty** gain influence over those who rely on logic and facts alone. The world does not reward truth; it rewards **conviction**.

Why Confidence Overrides Logic

The human brain is wired to **avoid uncertainty**. In an unpredictable world, people crave **strong, decisive leaders** who seem to have answers. Evolutionarily, uncertainty **meant danger**, while confidence **meant survival**. This bias still exists today, making us more likely to:

- Trust people who speak with certainty—even if they are wrong.
- Follow leaders who project unwavering conviction—even when their decisions are flawed.
- Doubt experts who express caution—even when they are right.

A 2013 study in the **Journal of Experimental Psychology** found that people rated **confident but incorrect individuals as more competent** than those who were accurate but hesitant. Even when presented with **objective evidence**, people gravitate toward those who express certainty rather than nuance.

This is why the most powerful manipulators—politicians, cult leaders, con artists—do not convince people with facts. They convince them with conviction.

The Confidence Effect in Action

To see how the **Illusion of Certainty** influences decisions, consider these real-world examples:

1. Politics: Certainty Wins Elections

Political debates are not won by **who presents the best facts**—they are won by **who sounds most certain**. A politician who **firmly states a falsehood** often appears **more credible** than an opponent who cautiously explains a complex truth.

Example:

- Politician A says: *"This policy will create 10,000 new jobs. That's a fact."*
- Politician B says: *"Well, based on economic trends, it is likely that job growth could occur, but there are many factors at play."*
- The audience perceives **Politician A as stronger**, even if their claim is unsupported.

Why? The brain values **certainty over accuracy** because certainty **feels like leadership.**

2. Sales & Persuasion: The Power of Absolute Statements

In sales, **a confident delivery sells more than product quality itself.** The best salespeople don't just describe a product's benefits—**they state them as undeniable truths.**

Example:

- A weak salesperson says: *"This could help improve your workflow."*
- A strong salesperson says: *"This will revolutionize how you work—no question about it."*
- Customers **gravitate toward the second approach**, even if both statements are about the same product.

Why? Certainty makes the brain feel **safe and decisive**, reducing doubt.

3. Social & Personal Influence: How Confidence Creates Authority

In social settings, those who **speak with certainty** are often seen as **leaders**, even when their knowledge is limited.

Example:

- At a party, someone says: *"This restaurant is the best in town. I guarantee it."*
- Another person says: *"I think it's supposed to be good, but I haven't tried all of them."*
- Most people will **trust and follow the first speaker's recommendation**, even though they provided no evidence.

This is why people who **speak in absolutes** ("always," "never," "definitely") are often **perceived as authorities**—even when they lack expertise.

How to Appear More Convincing—Even Without Expertise

If certainty **outweighs truth**, then mastering **how to project confidence** can instantly make you more persuasive. Here's how:

1. Speak in Absolutes

- Replace weak phrases like *"I think"* or *"it's possible"* with **direct statements**.
- Example: Instead of *"This might be a good idea,"* say, **"This is the best solution."**

2. Slow Down & Use Deliberate Pauses

- Rushed speech signals **uncertainty**, while **calm, deliberate speech signals authority.**
- Pausing before key statements **creates impact** and makes you seem in control.

3. Maintain Steady Eye Contact

- Looking away frequently suggests **doubt**.
- Holding eye contact while speaking **reinforces authority**.

4. Use Confident Body Language

- Stand **tall**, avoid nervous movements, and use **controlled gestures**.
- Leaning in slightly when making a point **amplifies certainty**.

These techniques make you **appear more knowledgeable and persuasive**, even in areas where you lack deep expertise.

Why People Reject Uncertainty—Even When It's the Truth

Despite the **Illusion of Certainty**, the real world is **full of complexity and unknowns**. However, the human mind **dislikes uncertainty**, which is why people:

- **Prefer simple lies over complex truths.**
- **Trust leaders who sound decisive—even if their decisions are reckless.**
- **Dismiss experts who say "it depends"—even when that's the honest answer.**

This explains why **conspiracy theories, fake news, and propaganda spread faster than nuanced facts**. People are not drawn to truth—they are drawn to **clarity and conviction**.

How to Defend Against Confidence-Based Manipulation

If confidence **can override truth**, how do you avoid being deceived by those who fake certainty?

- **Look Beyond Delivery** – Ask: *"Do they have evidence, or just confidence?"*
- **Beware of Absolute Language** – If someone says, *"This is the only way,"* question it.
- **Force Them to Explain** – Confident manipulators rely on vague claims. Asking *"Why?"* or *"How do you know?"* often exposes them.
- **Separate Feeling from Fact** – If something **feels true** just because it was said confidently, pause and analyze the logic.

Understanding the **Illusion of Certainty** allows you to **see through false confidence**—and use it to your advantage when needed.

Final Thought: Certainty Shapes Reality

People don't follow the smartest person in the room—they follow the one who sounds the most sure of themselves. Throughout history, leaders, influencers, and manipulators have understood that **certainty is more persuasive than truth**. When spoken with conviction, even a lie can spread faster than an honest but hesitant statement.

Mastering the illusion of certainty gives you an edge in every interaction. Whether in business, negotiations, leadership, or personal relationships, those who project confidence shape the reality of those around them. The ability to remove doubt from your voice, your body language, and your words makes others **see you as an authority—even before you prove yourself**.

Anchoring: Creating Emotional Associations for Influence

Anchoring is a psychological principle that links specific emotions, ideas, or behaviors to a stimulus, creating automatic responses when that stimulus is encountered again. This technique is widely used in sales, marketing, negotiation, leadership, and personal relationships to influence decision-making without direct persuasion. When applied correctly, anchoring forms strong subconscious associations, **making people react in predictable ways** without realizing they've been influenced.

How Anchoring Works: The Science of Mental Associations

The brain constantly forms connections between experiences, emotions, and external triggers. When a particular word, gesture, environment, or experience repeatedly occurs alongside an emotion, the brain automatically links them together.

A study by psychologists Daniel Kahneman and Amos Tversky in 1974 demonstrated anchoring in decision-making. Participants asked to estimate the number of African nations in the UN gave higher estimates when they were first exposed to a high random number, and lower estimates when they saw a lower number, even though the initial number had no actual relevance. This experiment proved that the brain latches onto the first piece of information it receives and uses it as a reference point for future judgments.

Influencers and manipulators use this principle to control perception, set expectations, and guide decisions by strategically introducing information that acts as a mental anchor.

Types of Anchoring and How to Use Them

1. Price Anchoring: Controlling Perceived Value

Anchoring is commonly used in sales and business negotiations to influence how people perceive value. When a high price is mentioned first, any lower price seems like a bargain. Conversely, when a low price is presented first, any higher price feels excessive.

A real estate agent might first show a luxury home listed at two million dollars before presenting a smaller home at one point two million dollars. The second home, which might have seemed expensive under normal conditions, now feels like a great deal in comparison.

Car dealerships apply the same principle by first showing a fully loaded model at fifty thousand dollars before presenting a base model at thirty-eight thousand dollars. After seeing the high-priced version, the second option appears more affordable.

This technique is also effective in salary negotiations. A job candidate who starts by mentioning a high salary expectation sets an anchor, making any lower counteroffer seem more reasonable. Similarly, a business negotiator who begins with an extreme demand can later appear cooperative by compromising at a more favorable point.

Starting with a high reference point creates an illusion of value, while beginning with a lower figure primes the target to expect minimal returns.

2. Emotional Anchoring: Linking Feelings to People and Places

People remember how they feel in a particular situation more than they remember the details of what was said. By consistently pairing an experience with a specific emotion, it is possible to create a subconscious link that triggers that feeling whenever the person encounters the same situation again.

A manager who consistently criticizes employees in a specific office space unintentionally anchors negative emotions to that location. Over time, employees may begin feeling anxious whenever they enter the room, even before anything has been said.

Conversely, a person who consistently makes others laugh and feel good in their presence becomes an anchor for positivity. Others will subconsciously seek out their company, associating them with happiness and comfort.

Locations also become emotional anchors. A couple who frequently visits a particular café during the early stages of their relationship may find that returning to that location in the future automatically triggers nostalgic emotions of warmth and connection.

By intentionally pairing presence with positive emotional experiences, it is possible to create lasting associations that influence how people feel about an individual or situation without their conscious awareness.

3. Physical Anchoring: Embedding Influence Through Touch and Movement

Physical sensations are powerful anchors because the brain links them directly to emotions and experiences. Public speakers, hypnotists, and leaders often use physical anchoring to reinforce ideas or create automatic responses.

A speaker who touches the podium every time they emphasize an important point conditions the audience to associate that movement with authority. Eventually, simply placing a hand on the podium can trigger a sense of importance in the audience's mind.

A coach or manager who offers a handshake or a pat on the back when delivering positive reinforcement anchors encouragement and motivation to that physical gesture. Over time, the individual receiving the feedback starts to experience confidence and validation whenever the same gesture is repeated.

This principle also applies in negative ways. If a parent or authority figure consistently raises their voice or invades someone's personal space when delivering criticism, the recipient may start feeling anxious whenever that person raises their voice, even in neutral situations.

Physical anchoring works best when it is repeated consistently over time, allowing the association to become automatic.

4. Verbal Anchoring: Using Language to Trigger Reactions

Words serve as anchors by triggering subconscious associations and setting expectations before a decision is even made.

A salesperson who repeatedly uses the phrase "limited-time opportunity" primes the brain to associate the offer with urgency, even if there is no real rush to buy. Similarly, a politician who consistently uses words like "freedom" and "security" in their speeches ensures that listeners automatically connect their policies with those positive concepts, even if the details do not align.

In personal relationships, people use verbal anchoring unconsciously. A manipulator who frequently tells their partner, "You always feel safe with me," is planting a subconscious connection between themselves and emotional security. Even if logical concerns arise later, the repeated verbal anchor reinforces trust and makes it harder to walk away.

Verbal anchoring is particularly effective when combined with emotional triggers. A leader who repeatedly emphasizes the word "growth" in discussions about company changes ensures that employees see transitions as opportunities rather than threats. A therapist who encourages clients to associate the phrase "calm and in control" with deep breathing techniques reinforces relaxation whenever those words are heard.

By carefully selecting repeated phrases, it is possible to shape how people interpret reality.

Advanced Anchoring: Strengthening and Reversing Associations

Anchoring does not happen instantly. The strongest anchors are built over multiple exposures, reinforcing the connection until it becomes an automatic response. The key to strengthening an anchor is **consistency and emotional intensity**.

A memory that carries a strong emotional charge, such as excitement, fear, or deep happiness, becomes an anchor much faster than neutral experiences. This is why people vividly remember where they were during significant historical events but may struggle to recall details of an average day.

When anchoring intentionally, the best approach is to attach a specific stimulus—whether a phrase, gesture, location, or physical touch—to a **strong emotion** that aligns with the desired outcome.

Conversely, unwanted anchors can be weakened or broken. If a person has developed an anxiety anchor in a specific setting, the best way to remove it is to repeatedly introduce **positive experiences** in that same environment. A person who associates public speaking with fear can slowly rewire their emotional response by practicing in low-pressure situations, gradually building new positive associations over time.

Breaking an anchor requires **interrupting the automatic response** and replacing it with a new one. If a manipulator has anchored someone to feel dependent on them, the target must actively introduce new, contrasting experiences that disconnect the manipulator from the anchored emotion.

How to Use Anchoring to Control Perception

Anchoring works because the brain forms automatic associations that bypass conscious analysis. A skilled influencer can take advantage of this by:

- Introducing a **high price first** to make lower prices seem more reasonable.
- Creating **emotional experiences** that link them to positive feelings.
- Using **physical and verbal anchors** to reinforce specific responses.
- Repeating key **words and gestures** until they trigger subconscious reactions.

Once an anchor is established, the target **will respond predictably to the stimulus**, often without realizing why.

By controlling what people associate with an experience, a person, or a decision, an influencer can **control how they think, feel, and react**—without ever needing to argue or persuade directly.

The Power of Strategic Silence

Silence is one of the most underrated tools in influence and manipulation. While most people associate power with speaking, those who understand how to use silence effectively can control conversations, negotiations, and even relationships without saying much at all.

Strategic silence creates discomfort, forces the other person to fill the gap, and subtly shifts control in any interaction. It is used in sales, leadership, interrogation tactics, and social dynamics to gain compliance and extract information without resistance.

This section explores how to use silence to increase authority, force concessions, and shape the thoughts of others while maintaining complete control.

Why Silence is So Powerful

The human brain is wired to seek patterns and fill in gaps. When a conversation has a pause, most people feel compelled to fill the silence with words—even if they didn't intend to speak.

This instinct creates a psychological advantage for those who understand how to use silence correctly. Strategic silence triggers three key effects:

1. **Discomfort and Pressure** – People naturally rush to fill silences, often revealing more than they intended.
2. **Perceived Authority** – Those who speak less appear more confident and powerful, while excessive talkers seem desperate.
3. **Amplified Impact** – When a statement is followed by silence, the brain processes it with greater significance.

These effects make silence one of the most effective influence techniques available, allowing a person to manipulate conversations without needing to say much at all.

How to Use Strategic Silence in Influence

1. The Power of the Pause

A well-timed pause **before or after** a statement increases its impact. The brain registers silence as an indication that something important was just said—or is about to be said.

- **Example (Public Speaking & Leadership)**
  A speaker who says, *"This is the most important decision you will ever make..."* and then pauses creates anticipation, forcing the audience to **focus completely on the next words.**
- **Example (Sales & Negotiation)**
  A salesperson who says, *"This deal is only available today..."* and then pauses makes the buyer feel pressure to respond, often leading to faster decisions.

Pauses give weight to words, making them seem more significant while forcing the listener to absorb them fully.

2. Using Silence to Extract Information

When people experience **a conversational silence, they feel compelled to speak just to fill the void**. This is why interrogators, journalists, and skilled negotiators use silence to get their targets to reveal more than they intended.

- **Example (Interrogation & Investigation)**
  A detective asks a suspect, *"Where were you last night?"* and after receiving an answer, simply stays silent while maintaining eye contact. The suspect, uncomfortable with the silence, may continue talking and inadvertently reveal additional details.
- **Example (Sales & Business Negotiations)**
  A buyer asks a salesperson, *"Is that the best price you can offer?"* When the salesperson does not immediately answer, the buyer, feeling the pressure of silence, might offer a lower counter before the seller even responds.

Silence creates an **urge to justify, explain, and negotiate against oneself**, making it a simple yet effective way to extract valuable information.

3. Forcing Concessions Without Speaking

When used correctly, silence forces the other person to concede or adjust their position without resistance.

- **Example (Job Negotiation)**
  A candidate is offered a salary of $80,000. Instead of responding immediately, they remain silent. The employer, feeling the discomfort of the silence, might add, *"...but we could go up to $85,000 if that makes a difference."*

- **Example (Sales Closing)**
  A customer asks for a discount. The salesperson responds, *"I can't offer a discount on this model..."* then stops talking. The customer, expecting an explanation, might say, *"Well, I guess I'll take it anyway."*

Silence after a demand creates pressure, often leading the other party to **compromise or concede without any additional persuasion needed**.

4. Establishing Dominance in Social and Business Settings

The person who speaks the least in a conversation **usually holds the most power**. Over-talking often signals nervousness, insecurity, or a need for validation. Silence, on the other hand, **projects confidence and authority**.

- **Example (Leadership & Authority)**
  A manager who pauses before responding to a question appears **thoughtful and decisive**, while one who speaks quickly may seem reactive or uncertain.

- **Example (Social Influence & Dating)**
  Someone who doesn't rush to respond to texts or pauses before answering questions seems more **in control, composed, and high-value**, increasing perceived status.

Silence is an unspoken display of power. Those who use it well often appear more intelligent, in control, and respected.

When to Break the Silence

While silence is powerful, **knowing when to break it is just as important**. If silence drags on too long, it can create unnecessary awkwardness or shift the balance too far in the other direction.

Break the silence when:

- The other person **becomes visibly uncomfortable** to the point of disengagement.
- The goal of extracting information or forcing a concession **has already been achieved**.
- It is **necessary to prevent losing rapport or creating negative tension**.

The key is to **let the silence work first**, then **speak only when necessary** to reinforce influence rather than weaken it.

How to Strengthen the Effect of Silence

Using silence effectively requires more than simply not speaking—it must be accompanied by the right **body language, tone, and timing** to maximize its effect.

1. Maintain Eye Contact

Looking away during silence weakens its effect. Holding eye contact increases tension and control, making the other person more likely to respond first.

2. Keep a Neutral or Confident Facial Expression

If silence is paired with an uncertain or uncomfortable look, it **signals weakness instead of strength**. Keeping a composed, neutral face ensures the silence works in your favor.

3. Use a Deliberate, Relaxed Posture

Fidgeting, shifting, or looking impatient weakens the power of silence. Remaining still and relaxed makes it clear that the silence is intentional and controlled.

4. Time the Pause Correctly

Pausing **too soon or too long** can disrupt the rhythm of a conversation. A **two- to four-second pause** is usually ideal for increasing impact without creating unnecessary awkwardness.

By pairing silence with **confident non-verbal cues**, it becomes an even more powerful tool for influence.

Real-World Applications of Strategic Silence

- **Sales & Business:** After making a proposal, stay silent and let the other party respond first.
- **Negotiations:** When asked to justify a demand, pause instead of explaining—this often forces the other side to justify their own position instead.
- **Leadership & Public Speaking:** Use intentional pauses to emphasize key points, project authority, and make statements more impactful.
- **Dating & Social Influence:** Avoid over-explaining or rushing to fill pauses in conversation—this increases attraction by making interactions feel more natural and controlled.

Silence is one of the easiest yet most powerful influence tools because it **requires no effort but yields significant results**.

Final Thought: The Less You Say, the More Power You Hold

Strategic silence works because **people expect conversations to be continuous**. When silence interrupts that rhythm, the brain interprets it as a signal that something important is happening.

By mastering silence, it becomes possible to:

- Extract more information than the other person intended to give.
- Increase perceived authority and confidence.
- Force concessions and agreement without direct persuasion.
- Amplify the impact of words when they are spoken.

The ability to **control when to speak and when to remain silent** is a skill that **separates average influencers from master manipulators**.

The Yes-Ladder Technique: Creating a Pattern of Agreement

The Yes-Ladder technique is one of the most effective psychological strategies for influence. It works by guiding a person through **a series of small agreements**, gradually increasing their willingness to comply with larger requests. By getting someone to say "yes" repeatedly, you create a psychological pattern that makes them far more likely to agree to bigger commitments—without realizing they are being led.

This technique is widely used in **sales, negotiations, persuasion, and even personal relationships** to shape decisions in a way that feels completely natural to the target.

Why the Yes-Ladder Works: The Psychology of Commitment

Human behavior is strongly driven by **consistency and commitment**. When people make a choice, they subconsciously align their future actions to remain consistent with that decision.

Psychologists Robert Cialdini and Jonathan Freedman demonstrated this in a famous 1966 study. Researchers asked homeowners if they would place a large, ugly "Drive Safely" sign on their front lawn. Most declined. However, when a different group was **first asked to put a small sticker in their window** supporting safe driving, they were **far more likely to later agree to the large sign**—even though the request was much bigger.

The small, initial agreement **established an identity** in the target's mind. Since they had already committed to supporting safe driving, rejecting the larger request would have felt inconsistent with their past decision.

This principle is the foundation of the Yes-Ladder. Once someone **starts saying yes**, they are psychologically conditioned to **keep saying yes**.

How to Use the Yes-Ladder for Influence

1. Start with a Low-Commitment Request

The first "yes" should be **small, easy, and non-threatening**. The goal is to get the target to agree to something **without feeling pressured**.

- **Example (Sales & Marketing)**
  A website might offer a free newsletter signup. Once a person agrees to receive emails, they are more likely to later buy a product because they have already said yes to engagement.
- **Example (Personal Influence & Relationships)**
  Instead of asking someone out directly, a smoother approach would be, *"Want to grab a quick coffee?"* Once they say yes to a small meeting, it becomes easier to escalate to a dinner date later.

Once a person **has made an initial commitment**, their subconscious desire to stay **consistent** makes them more receptive to the next request.

2. Build on the First Yes with Slightly Larger Requests

Once the target has agreed to the first step, gradually increase the level of commitment. Each new "yes" should feel like **a natural progression** from the last one.

- **Example (Negotiation & Business Deals)**
  If a client is hesitant to agree to a full deal, start by asking them to agree to **a minor term or a free trial**.
- **Example (Social Influence & Leadership)**
  If you want an employee to take on a major responsibility, first get them to say yes to **a small task related to that responsibility**. Once they complete it, they are more likely to accept a bigger role.

The key is **incremental agreement**. Each small step leads seamlessly to the next, reinforcing the pattern of compliance.

3. Use Momentum to Secure the Final Agreement

By the time a person has said yes multiple times, they are psychologically primed to say yes to **the ultimate request**—even if it is something they initially would have resisted.

- **Example (Sales Closing)**
  A salesperson first gets a customer to say yes to a free demo. Then they ask if the customer sees value in the product. Finally, they ask if the customer wants to sign up. By this point, saying no feels inconsistent with the previous yes answers.
- **Example (Social Manipulation & Persuasion)**
  A skilled influencer may first ask for **a small favor**, like borrowing a pen. Then, they escalate to asking for a minor task. Eventually, they make a much bigger request, which is now harder to refuse.

At this stage, the target often **feels obligated** to agree, as rejecting the final request would contradict their previous behavior.

Advanced Strategies to Strengthen the Yes-Ladder

1. Use Questions That Lead to "Yes" Automatically

Some questions are designed to **make no sense to reject**. These are known as **leading questions** because they **guide** the target toward agreement.

- **Example (Sales & Marketing)**
  A salesperson might ask, *"Would you like to save money on your bills?"* The automatic answer is yes. The next question might be, *"Would you like to see how this product can help?"*—which now feels like a logical step forward.
- **Example (Personal Influence & Social Dynamics)**
  Instead of asking, *"Want to help me with this project?"* say, *"Wouldn't it be great if we got this project done more efficiently?"* This makes agreement feel like the only reasonable response.

Framing questions so that the answer is **always yes** increases compliance before the person even realizes they are being led.

2. Combine the Yes-Ladder with Social Proof

Social proof—showing that others have already agreed—makes people even more likely to say yes.

- **Example (Sales & Negotiation)**
  A marketer might say, *"Most people in your situation have already signed up for this service. Would you like to see why?"* This primes the brain to assume saying yes is the expected behavior.
- **Example (Persuasion & Group Influence)**
  A speaker might say, *"Raise your hand if you agree that personal growth is important."* Once hands are raised, the audience is conditioned to agree with the next statements as well.

When people see **others saying yes**, their own willingness to comply increases.

3. Use Emotional Priming Before the Yes-Ladder

People are more likely to say yes when they are in **a positive emotional state**. Setting the right emotional tone before starting the Yes-Ladder increases its effectiveness.

- **Example (Personal Relationships & Influence)**
  If someone is laughing and feeling relaxed, they are **more likely to agree to a favor** than if they were stressed or annoyed.
- **Example (Sales & Business Negotiation)**
  Before making a request, a salesperson might engage in **small talk about something positive** to get the client into an agreeable mindset.

Priming the brain with positive emotions makes each yes feel **more natural and automatic**.

How to Defend Against the Yes-Ladder

While the Yes-Ladder is highly effective, it can also be used against you. Recognizing the technique helps to prevent **unconscious compliance**.

To resist:

- **Be aware of small agreements that lead to bigger commitments.**
  Just because you said yes to something minor doesn't mean you have to say yes to the next request.
- **Pause before agreeing to the next step.** If you feel momentum pushing you forward, take a moment to ask, *"Do I actually want this?"*

▶ **Break the pattern.** If someone is leading you through multiple yes responses, consciously say no to disrupt the psychological flow.

Understanding how the technique works allows you to **stay in control of your decisions** rather than being led without realizing it.

Final Thought: The Path to Influence is Built on Small Agreements

The Yes-Ladder works because people strive for **consistency**. Once someone starts saying yes, they unconsciously want to maintain that pattern, making them more susceptible to bigger requests.

By mastering this technique, it becomes possible to:

- Get people to **agree to things they would normally resist**
- Make compliance feel **natural and self-driven**
- Increase influence in **sales, leadership, social situations, and personal relationships**

Most importantly, the Yes-Ladder **makes persuasion feel effortless**—because the target believes every decision was their own.

CHAPTER 4
SOCIAL ENGINEERING – THE TACTICS OF CON ARTISTS & INTELLIGENCE AGENCIES

Social engineering is the **art of deception**—the ability to manipulate people into giving up information, making decisions, or taking actions they normally wouldn't. Unlike hacking, which targets systems, social engineering **targets the human mind**, exploiting trust, authority, and cognitive biases to achieve a desired outcome.

This chapter reveals the psychological tricks used by **scammers, spies, hackers, and con artists** to manipulate people without them realizing it. These techniques are used in **identity fraud, corporate espionage, political influence, and even everyday social manipulation**.

By understanding these tactics, you will not only recognize when they are being used against you but also learn how to apply them for **influence, persuasion, and control** in business, leadership, and personal interactions.

The Pretext Method: Creating Stories That Build Trust Instantly

The **Pretext Method** is one of the most powerful tools in social engineering. It relies on creating a **believable story, role, or scenario** to gain someone's trust and manipulate their behavior. This technique is used by **scammers, spies, intelligence agencies, and con artists** to infiltrate secure environments, extract sensitive information, and influence people without resistance.

A strong pretext convinces the target that the manipulator is someone they should **trust, obey, or assist**. The key to this method's success lies in the psychological principle of **contextual acceptance**—people naturally accept information when it fits into a **logical, believable framework**.

This section explores how **pretexting works**, why it is so effective, and how to construct convincing **identities, stories, and roles** to influence others without them realizing they are being manipulated.

Why the Pretext Method Works: The Power of Contextual Acceptance

The human brain is wired to **trust and cooperate with people who fit expected roles**. If someone claims to be a doctor, an IT technician, or a law enforcement officer, most people instinctively comply with their requests—especially if the pretext is backed by **confidence, familiarity, and supporting details**.

This works because:

1. **People don't question what seems normal.** If an action or request fits into a familiar **context**, the brain automatically **accepts it without deep analysis**.
2. **Authority and legitimacy create compliance.** A well-crafted pretext makes people **feel obligated** to follow instructions.
3. **Information overload weakens suspicion.** When a target is given **too much contextual information**, they often default to **trusting the source** rather than analyzing inconsistencies.

A manipulator who understands these principles can construct **realistic pretexts** that lower suspicion and increase cooperation.

How to Create a Convincing Pretext

1. Establish a Believable Identity

The first step in a successful pretext is **creating an identity that fits the situation**. The role must align with the target's expectations to **reduce skepticism and increase compliance**.

- **Example (Corporate Espionage):** A social engineer **poses as an IT technician**, claiming to need access to an employee's computer to install updates.

- **Example (Financial Scams):** A scammer **pretends to be a bank employee**, warning the victim about "suspicious activity" and requesting account verification.
- **Example (Relationship Manipulation):** A manipulator **pretends to be deeply interested** in someone's hobbies or struggles to build fast trust and connection.

A good pretext creates an immediate sense of **familiarity and legitimacy**, making the target more likely to cooperate.

2. Use Specific Details to Add Authenticity

A vague identity raises suspicion, but a **detailed pretext** creates believability. Details **bypass critical thinking** by making the story feel real.

- Instead of saying, *"I'm from IT,"* say,
    - *"I'm from the IT security team in building C, handling server updates for encrypted login access."*
- Instead of, *"I work with your bank,"* say,
    - *"I'm Jonathan from the fraud prevention unit at Chase Bank, handling a potential security breach on your account ending in 4582."*

The more specific the details, the less likely the target is to question the story.

3. Create a Sense of Urgency or Importance

Most successful pretexts include **an element of urgency**. When people feel pressured, they think **less critically** and act on **instinct**.

- **Example (Hacking & Social Engineering):**
    - *"We need to verify your credentials immediately, or your company login will be locked for security reasons."*
- **Example (Scamming & Fraud):**
    - *"There has been a data breach in your account. To protect your funds, please confirm your identity now."*

By manufacturing urgency, the manipulator prevents the target from **stopping to analyze the request**.

4. Leverage Authority & Trust Signals

Authority plays a critical role in pretexting. People are conditioned to comply with **figures of authority** without questioning them.

- **Example (Impersonation Scams):**
    - *A scammer calls a victim, claiming to be from "the IRS" and demands immediate payment to avoid legal action.*
- **Example (Corporate Security Breaches):**
    - *A hacker **dresses in a company's uniform** and walks into a secure facility, pretending to be a contractor with urgent repairs.*

To reinforce credibility, manipulators often use **props, official-sounding jargon, and psychological pressure** to make their pretext **irresistible**.

5. Build an Emotional Connection

Some pretexts are effective because they **exploit emotions** rather than authority. When a person feels an emotional connection, they are far less likely to question a request.

- **Example (Romance Scams):**
    - *A scammer builds an emotional relationship with the target before asking for financial help due to an "emergency."*
- **Example (Influence & Deception in Friendships):**
    - *A manipulator gains trust by sharing a personal secret, encouraging the target to reciprocate and lower their defenses.*

Once trust and emotional connection are established, the target **willingly** provides information or assistance without suspecting manipulation.

Real-World Applications of the Pretext Method

Corporate Espionage & Cybersecurity Breaches

Hackers use pretexting to bypass security protocols by **convincing employees to grant access** through fake IT support calls or impersonating executives.

Personal & Social Manipulation

In relationships and social circles, pretexting is used to **gain influence, extract secrets, and control decision-making** by playing the role of a trusted advisor or confidant.

How to Defend Against Pretexting Manipulation

- **Verify identities before providing any sensitive information.** If someone claims to be from a company, **call the company directly** to confirm.
- **Be suspicious of urgent requests.** Most real businesses and authorities do not demand **immediate action under pressure**.
- **Ask unexpected questions.** A legitimate person will answer with confidence, but a manipulator may hesitate or contradict themselves.
- **Limit the amount of personal information shared online.** Pretext manipulators often **research targets in advance** to craft convincing backstories.

Recognizing pretexting techniques makes it possible to **question suspicious requests, slow down interactions, and maintain control** in any situation.

Final Thought: Why the Pretext Method is So Dangerous

Pretexting works because it **exploits trust, authority, and psychological shortcuts** that people rely on in daily life. The most effective manipulators **don't force compliance—they create scenarios where the target willingly cooperates**.

Mastering this technique allows an influencer to:

- Bypass skepticism and gain instant trust.
- Extract valuable information without resistance.
- Control conversations and interactions with ease.

Understanding how pretexting works is the first step in **both using and defending against** this form of manipulation.

The Illusion of Morality: How Ethics Are Used to Manipulate

Most people believe that their actions are guided by **personal ethics**, a sense of right and wrong that defines their choices. But morality is not an objective force—it is a **constructed tool**, often shaped and weaponized by those in power to control others. Whether through **politics, religion, media, or social expectations**, morality is one of the most powerful levers of influence, used to justify **obedience, compliance, and even oppression.**

In reality, people do not act based on a universal moral code. They act based on **what they have been conditioned to believe is moral**. The difference between a freedom fighter and a terrorist is not their actions—it is the label that society assigns to them. The difference between a hero and a criminal is often **who gets to write history**. Those who understand **how morality is framed and manipulated** can control how people **think, act, and judge**—without them ever realizing they were influenced.

Why People Comply with Moral Authority

Humans are deeply wired to seek **social acceptance and moral validation**. From childhood, we are conditioned to associate **obedience with goodness** and **defiance with wrongdoing**. This makes morality a powerful **tool for influence**, because:

- **People fear being perceived as immoral** – Nobody wants to be the "bad guy."
- **Guilt and shame are more powerful than logic** – A moral argument can override reason.
- **Society rewards those who align with moral norms** – Breaking moral expectations leads to social exile.

Because morality is so deeply ingrained in identity, those who **control the definition of morality** control the **behavior of others**. Governments, religions, and corporations have long understood this—shaping moral narratives to **justify actions, suppress dissent, and create compliance.**

Moral Manipulation in Action

Morality has been **one of the most effective control mechanisms in history**. By shaping what people believe is right or wrong, those in power can **steer entire societies without force**. Here are some of the most common tactics used to manipulate morality:

1. Moral Licensing – The Illusion of Being "Good" Justifies Harm

Moral licensing is when people **justify unethical behavior** because they believe they have already acted morally. This is why someone who donates to charity may later **feel justified in cutting ethical corners** in business. The mind **keeps a subconscious "moral balance sheet,"** and manipulators use this to their advantage.

- **Example (Corporate Ethics Washing):**
    - A company engages in unethical labor practices but promotes its **environmental donations** to maintain a "good" image.
    - Consumers feel comfortable supporting them because they have been framed as **morally responsible**.

- **Example (Personal Manipulation):**
    - A person says, *"After all I've done for you, how can you not help me with this?"*
    - They frame past good deeds as justification for present demands.

By understanding **moral licensing**, manipulators create **an illusion of ethical superiority** that allows them to act without consequences.

2. The "Good vs. Evil" Fallacy – Simplifying Complex Morality for Control

Most people prefer **black-and-white thinking** over moral complexity. Those in power use this **cognitive bias** to divide people into **heroes and villains**, making manipulation easier.

- **Example (Political Propaganda):**
    - Governments frame their enemies as **evil and dangerous**, while their own actions are always **righteous and necessary**.
    - Citizens then **support extreme actions** (wars, censorship, oppression) because they believe they are defending morality.

- **Example (Social Control):**
  - A leader tells their followers, *"Anyone who questions me is against us."*
  - This forces blind loyalty, making independent thinking feel like **betrayal**.

The **good vs. evil illusion** prevents critical thinking by making people **emotionally invested in a simplified narrative.**

3. Manufactured Outrage – Controlling People by Triggering Moral Emotion

Outrage is a **fast-track to influence**. When people feel morally offended, they **lose logical reasoning and act on impulse**. This is why outrage is one of the most commonly used manipulation tactics.

- **Example (Media & Clickbait Culture):**
  - News outlets manufacture outrage by exaggerating **social issues or political scandals**.
  - People become emotionally invested, driving engagement, division, and compliance.

- **Example (Corporate & Social Agendas):**
  - A company frames **a competitor or critic as unethical**, shifting attention away from their own issues.
  - People instinctively side with the "morally correct" option—even if it was manufactured.

Outrage **short-circuits logical thinking** and makes people **easier to control** because they react emotionally rather than analytically.

4. Fear of Social Rejection – Using Morality to Enforce Groupthink

Humans are tribal by nature, and **fear of social rejection** is a strong motivator. When moral narratives are used as **weapons of conformity**, people comply out of **fear of exile** rather than genuine belief.

- **Example (Religious & Cultural Conditioning):**
  - People are taught that questioning beliefs leads to punishment or exclusion.
  - This discourages independent thought and reinforces moral obedience.

- **Example (Corporate & Workplace Manipulation):**
  - Employees are pressured to **adopt company culture and values**, even if they disagree.
  - Dissent is punished by **loss of promotions, opportunities, or social acceptance**.

By linking **morality to belonging**, manipulators **create self-policing populations** who conform out of **fear, not agreement**.

How to Defend Against Moral Manipulation

Since morality is **deeply tied to identity and emotion**, it is difficult to recognize when it's being used as a control mechanism. The key to resisting moral manipulation is to **question the source, logic, and intent behind moral arguments**.

1. Question Who Defines Morality

Whenever someone claims an action is "right" or "wrong," ask:

- *"Who benefits if I believe this?"*
- *"Is this an absolute truth or a socially constructed rule?"*

Many moral claims are not about **ethics**—they are about **control**.

2. Recognize When Outrage is Manufactured

If a news story, social movement, or leader is **pushing extreme moral emotion**, ask:

- *"Is this real injustice, or am I being manipulated into feeling a certain way?"*
- *"Is there an incentive behind this outrage?"*

If something **triggers an instant emotional reaction**, slow down and analyze before engaging.

3. Beware of Forced Group Morality

If a group **punishes independent thinking**, it is likely using **morality as a control tool**. Ask yourself:

- *"Am I agreeing because I believe this, or because I fear rejection?"*
- *"Would I still hold this belief if I were in a different social environment?"*

True morality should withstand independent thought, not require blind conformity.

Final Thought: Morality is a Double-Edged Sword

Morality is one of the most **powerful forces in human psychology**. It can inspire greatness, create order, and unite people under common values. But it can also be **manipulated to justify oppression, silence dissent, and control entire societies**.

Those who understand **how morality is shaped, framed, and enforced** gain the ability to **see beyond false narratives and resist emotional control**. The question is not whether morality is being used as a weapon—it is **whether you recognize it when it happens**.

The Illusion of Consensus: How Group Pressure Shapes Decisions

Humans like to believe they are **independent thinkers**, capable of forming their own judgments and making rational choices. But the truth is, most people do not make decisions based on **logic** or **facts**—they make decisions based on **what they believe everyone else is doing**.

The illusion of consensus is one of the most **powerful tools of social manipulation**. When people perceive an idea, belief, or behavior as **widely accepted**, they are far more likely to **adopt it themselves**—even if they originally disagreed. Manipulators understand this and **manufacture the appearance of mass agreement** to pressure individuals into compliance.

From **politics to marketing, cults to corporations**, the ability to **create false consensus** gives those in power the ability to **control what people believe, how they act, and what they think is "normal."**

Why People Follow the Crowd

The brain is wired for **social conformity**. Throughout history, human survival depended on **group belonging**—ostracization from the tribe meant **death**. Because of this, our minds have evolved to:

- **Trust the majority** – If most people believe something, the brain assumes it must be true.
- **Fear standing out** – Going against the group triggers anxiety and social rejection.
- **Seek validation** – People subconsciously **mirror** group behavior to fit in.

This is why the **illusion of mass agreement** is so dangerous. If people believe "everyone thinks this way," they are far less likely to **question, resist, or think critically**.

Manipulators use this **psychological weakness** to **control entire populations without force**.

The Bandwagon Effect: Why Consensus Feels Like Truth

The Bandwagon Effect is a cognitive bias where people adopt beliefs simply because they believe others already believe them. This is why:

- **Trends spread so quickly** (even when they make no sense).
- **Political movements gain momentum** (even when their claims are unproven).
- **Businesses use fake reviews and testimonials** (because people assume a popular product must be good).

Example: Political & Social Influence

- Politicians manipulate **poll results, crowd sizes, and media coverage** to create the illusion of overwhelming support.
- People assume the "majority" agrees, even when it is a **carefully crafted perception**.

Example: Marketing & Sales Tactics

- ▶ Companies use phrases like **"Bestseller," "Most Popular," and "#1 Choice"** to make products seem universally accepted.
- ▶ Consumers assume high sales **must mean the product is good**, even when those numbers are **inflated or fabricated**.

This bias makes people **ignore their own doubts and blindly follow the perceived majority**—even when that **majority doesn't actually exist**.

False Consensus Manipulation: Manufacturing Agreement

The most effective manipulators don't just **exploit existing trends**—they **create the illusion of consensus** to push an agenda.

How False Consensus is Created

1. Control the Narrative

- ▶ If **all major media outlets** repeat the same message, people assume it must be true.
- ▶ If **only one side of a debate is visible**, people assume there is no valid opposition.

2. Flood the Space with Repetition

- ▶ Social media bots, paid influencers, and fake reviews create an artificial sense of popularity.
- ▶ Repeated exposure to an idea makes the brain more likely to accept it as truth.

3. Silence Dissenters

- ▶ Those who **question or challenge** the narrative are framed as "extremists," "misinformed," or "dangerous."
- ▶ People fear **social backlash**, so they remain silent—even if they disagree.

When people **only see one viewpoint**, they assume **everyone agrees**—so they conform without question.

How Cults, Movements, and Political Groups Enforce Compliance

Throughout history, the illusion of consensus has been used to **control populations and suppress opposition**.

- **Cults:** Members are told, "Everyone here agrees with this. If you don't, something must be wrong with you."
- **Authoritarian Regimes:** Governments use **state-controlled media** to make it seem like **100% of the population supports them**.
- **Corporate Environments:** Employees are pressured into aligning with **company culture and ideology**, fearing exclusion if they disagree.

By making people **afraid to speak up**, manipulators create **self-policing populations** that enforce conformity **without requiring external force**.

How to Resist Groupthink and Maintain Independent Judgment

Because **social pressure is so powerful**, resisting **false consensus manipulation** requires conscious effort. Here's how to **break free** from groupthink:

1. Question the Source of Consensus

- Ask yourself: *"Am I seeing real widespread agreement, or just controlled messaging?"*
- Look for **dissenting opinions**—if they are being **silenced or ridiculed**, manipulation is at play.

2. Beware of "Everyone Agrees" Language

- Statements like *"The science is settled," "There's no debate,"* or *"Everyone knows this"* are red flags.
- If someone discourages questions, **question them even more**.

3. Recognize When Fear is Being Used to Enforce Compliance

- If disagreement triggers accusations of ignorance, hate, or extremism, ask yourself:
    - *"Is this person arguing with facts, or just using emotional pressure?"*

4. Seek Uncensored Discussions

- ▸ Follow people who **challenge mainstream narratives**, even if you don't agree with them.
- ▸ Be willing to **consider opposing views** without emotional bias.

The **easiest way to control people** is to make them **afraid to disagree**. Those who resist this fear become immune to false consensus manipulation.

Final Thought: The Most Dangerous Lies Are the Ones Everyone Believes

The illusion of consensus is **a powerful form of control**—not because people are forced to comply, but because they **willingly follow the perceived majority**. Most will never stop to ask, *"Is this really what everyone believes? Or is this just what I've been shown?"*

True independence is not about rejecting **all popular opinions**—it's about recognizing **when consensus is real, and when it has been manufactured**. The ability to **question the illusion of mass agreement** separates those who think for themselves from those who are simply **following the crowd**.

Emotional Hijacking: Controlling Actions by Triggering Feelings

Emotions override logic. When a person is **overwhelmed by strong emotions**, their ability to think critically diminishes, making them far more susceptible to manipulation. Emotional hijacking occurs when **a manipulator intentionally triggers specific emotions**—such as fear, excitement, guilt, or anger—to override rational thinking and control decision-making.

This technique is used in **politics, marketing, relationships, negotiations, and cult influence** to steer people into actions they might **normally resist**. By understanding how emotional hijacking works, it becomes possible to **use it for influence—or defend against it when someone else is trying to manipulate you**.

Why Emotional Hijacking Works: The Brain Under Stress

The brain has two primary processing systems:

1. **The Logical Mind (Prefrontal Cortex)** – Processes facts, makes rational decisions, and weighs risks.
2. **The Emotional Mind (Limbic System & Amygdala)** – Reacts to threats, rewards, and emotions instinctively.

When emotions run high, the **logical mind is overpowered** by the emotional brain, causing **impulse-driven decisions**. This is known as the **Amygdala Hijack**, a term coined by psychologist Daniel Goleman. When this happens, a person:

- Becomes **hyper-focused** on their emotions, ignoring logical analysis.
- Reacts **instinctively** rather than thinking critically.
- Becomes **highly suggestible**, making them easy to manipulate.

By triggering strong emotions, a manipulator can **steer thoughts and actions** without needing to provide logical reasoning.

How Emotional Hijacking is Used to Control People

1. Using Fear to Override Rational Thinking

Fear is the **most powerful** emotional trigger because it **shuts down logical analysis** and triggers **survival instincts**. When afraid, people seek immediate safety, making them **more compliant and easier to control**.

- **Example (Political Manipulation & Propaganda):**
    - Governments and media outlets **exaggerate threats** (terrorism, economic collapse, crime) to make citizens support **strict policies, surveillance, or war**.
- **Example (Sales & Marketing):**
    - Insurance companies use fear-based messaging:
        - *"What happens to your family if you die unexpectedly? Make sure they're protected."*
    - The fear of loss **pushes customers to buy** without deep analysis.

- Example (Relationship & Social Control):
    - A manipulative partner might say:
        - *"If you leave me, no one else will ever love you."*
    - The **fear of abandonment** forces emotional compliance.

Fear **creates urgency**, making people **act impulsively** to avoid perceived danger.

2. Triggering Guilt to Control Behavior

Guilt is a powerful weapon in manipulation. When a person **feels responsible for someone else's suffering**, they become willing to **comply with demands to relieve their guilt**.

- Example (Family & Personal Relationships):
    - A parent tells their child:
        - *"After everything I've done for you, this is how you repay me?"*
    - The guilt forces the child to **act against their own interests** to seek approval.
- Example (Religious & Social Influence):
    - Religious leaders frame moral choices as:
        - *"If you don't donate, you are turning your back on your community."*
    - The fear of **moral failure** forces compliance.
- Example (Workplace Manipulation):
    - A boss says to an overworked employee:
        - *"We're counting on you—you wouldn't let the team down, would you?"*
    - The guilt prevents the employee from setting boundaries or refusing extra work.

Guilt bypasses logical reasoning by making the **target feel obligated** to act.

3. Exploiting Excitement to Push Quick Decisions

Excitement overrides skepticism. When people are **emotionally high**, they act **on impulse** and ignore warning signs.

- **Example (High-Stakes Sales & Investment Scams):**
    - Scammers create excitement:
        - *"This is a once-in-a-lifetime opportunity! Get in now before it's too late!"*
    - The **adrenaline rush** suppresses logical thinking, leading to reckless decisions.

- **Example (Relationships & Love Bombing):**
    - A manipulator overwhelms a new romantic partner with:
        - *Excessive compliments, gifts, and promises of a future together.*
    - The target becomes **emotionally hooked**, making it harder to see red flags.

- **Example (Marketing & Luxury Branding):**
    - Brands use exclusivity to generate excitement:
        - *"Only the elite wear this brand—join the luxury class today."*
    - The emotional appeal makes people spend irrationally.

Excitement creates **a temporary emotional high**, making targets act before they have time to evaluate the decision logically.

4. Using Anger to Create Division & Control Perception

Anger is one of the **easiest emotions to manipulate** because it **shuts down rational discussion** and **fuels tribalism**. When people are angry, they become **reactionary, irrational, and more likely to follow commands**.

- **Example (Political Manipulation & Divide-and-Conquer Tactics):**
    - Politicians **blame an opposing group** for societal problems:
    - *"It's their fault you're suffering!"*
    - The target audience **redirects their frustration** at the chosen scapegoat instead of questioning leadership.

- **Example (Workplace Power Plays):**
    - A boss creates rivalry between employees so they compete instead of challenging management.

- **Example (Relationship & Social Manipulation):**
    - A toxic friend whispers:
    - *"Did you hear what they said about you? You shouldn't trust them."*
    - This creates division, making the target more dependent on the manipulator.

Anger **clouds judgment** and makes people **easier to direct** toward a specific target or action.

How to Defend Against Emotional Hijacking

1. Recognize When Your Emotions Are Being Manipulated

If a situation suddenly **makes you feel intense fear, guilt, excitement, or anger**, stop and ask:

- *"Am I being emotionally manipulated?"*
- *"Is this urgency real, or is someone creating pressure?"*

Strong emotions **should be a red flag** that critical thinking is being **bypassed**.

2. Delay Decisions Until Emotions Settle

Emotional hijacking **relies on impulsive action**. To regain control:

- **Take a step back** and refuse to make a decision while feeling emotional.
- **Wait at least 24 hours** before acting on any major decision.
- **Ask for a second opinion** from someone outside the situation.

Time allows emotions to settle, giving the **logical brain time to re-engage**.

3. Challenge the Narrative Being Presented

Emotional manipulation often **frames reality in a specific way** to push a desired outcome.

To break the illusion:

- **Question the source:** *"Why are they making me feel this way? What do they gain?"*
- **Consider alternative viewpoints:** *"What if I'm only seeing one side of the story?"*
- **Seek independent verification:** *"Are there facts supporting this, or is it just emotion-driven?"*

A logical analysis of the situation weakens emotional control.

Final Thought: The Power of Emotional Hijacking in Control

Emotional hijacking is **a very effective manipulation tool** because it overrides **logic, skepticism, and independent thought**.

By triggering **fear, guilt, excitement, or anger**, manipulators can:

- **Force compliance without direct persuasion.**
- **Make people act against their own best interests.**
- **Create long-term loyalty, division, or dependency.**

Mastering this technique allows an influencer to **steer decisions and perceptions** effortlessly—while making the target believe they are acting **out of free will**.

CHAPTER 5

THE DARK SIDE – HOW MANIPULATION IS USED IN THE REAL WORLD

Manipulation isn't just a concept—it is actively shaping **business, politics, social media, and personal relationships** every day. Some of the most influential figures and organizations in the world use psychological manipulation to **control perception, influence behavior, and increase power**.

This chapter exposes **real-world examples of manipulation in action**, revealing how advertising, propaganda, and social engineering shape the way people think, feel, and act—often without them realizing it.

By understanding these tactics, it becomes easier to recognize when manipulation is **being used against you**, and how to **resist or counteract** it in daily life.

Advertising & Marketing: The Science of Consumer Control

Advertising is **not about selling products**—it is about **selling ideas, emotions, and desires** that make people believe they need those products. Every major brand uses **psychological triggers** to manipulate consumers into making purchases, often **against their own rational judgment**.

From **fear-based messaging to artificial scarcity, status symbols, and social proof**, this section breaks down the psychological tactics businesses use to **control consumer behavior**—and how to recognize when you're being influenced.

How Advertising Manipulates Perception

The brain is not a logical decision-maker—it relies on **emotional and subconscious triggers** to determine what is valuable. Advertisers **bypass logical thinking** by using psychological strategies that make a product **irresistible** without needing actual merit.

The key principles used in marketing manipulation are:

1. **Emotional Triggers:** Ads don't sell products; they sell feelings (security, status, belonging).
2. **Cognitive Biases:** People buy impulsively based on scarcity, fear of missing out, and authority cues.
3. **Repetition & Familiarity:** The more you see a brand, the more trustworthy it feels—regardless of quality.

These principles are deliberately **engineered** to make consumers believe they are making **free choices**, when in reality, they are being subtly directed toward a **pre-determined outcome**.

Psychological Manipulation Tactics Used in Advertising

1. Fear-Based Marketing: Selling Protection Against Manufactured Threats

Fear is one of the most powerful motivators. Advertisers create **problems or insecurities** in people's minds—then sell a solution.

- **Example (Beauty & Skincare Industry):**
    - *"Are wrinkles making you look older than you are?"*
    - The ad first creates **anxiety about aging**, then offers an anti-aging cream as the only solution.
- **Example (Security & Insurance Companies):**
    - *"Cybercrime is increasing—do you have the right protection?"*
    - The ad instills **fear of loss**, making the target act out of **panic instead of logic**.

Fear-based advertising **manipulates perception** by making the consumer believe they are **at risk**, forcing them to take immediate action.

2. Scarcity & Urgency: Forcing Quick Buying Decisions

By making a product seem **limited**, advertisers **create artificial demand**—pushing consumers to buy before they even think about whether they truly want it.

- **Example (Online Shopping & E-commerce):**
    - "Only 3 left in stock!"
    - This **triggers urgency**, making the consumer buy impulsively to avoid missing out.

- **Example (Luxury & High-Status Brands):**
    - "Exclusive, limited edition release."
    - Even if the product **isn't truly rare**, the **illusion of exclusivity** makes people desire it more.

Scarcity creates **perceived value**, increasing willingness to pay higher prices—even when logical analysis would suggest otherwise.

3. The Halo Effect: Associating Brands with High-Status Figures

The **Halo Effect** occurs when a brand is associated with **a celebrity, athlete, or authority figure**, making it appear **superior without actual merit**.

- **Example (Sports Sponsorships & Celebrity Endorsements):**
    - "Cristiano Ronaldo uses this shampoo—so should you."
    - The brand becomes **automatically linked** to elite performance and success, even though **Ronaldo's hair has nothing to do with the product's quality**.

- **Example (Political & Business Leaders Using High-Status Affiliations):**
    - A politician **appears next to a popular public figure**, implying endorsement without explicitly stating it.

People **transfer positive emotions** from the **figure to the brand**, increasing **trust and desirability** without needing real evidence.

THE DARK SIDE – HOW MANIPULATION IS USED IN THE REAL WORLD

4. Social Proof: The Herd Mentality in Consumer Behavior

People assume that **if others are doing something, it must be the right choice**. Advertisers use this to manipulate consumers into **following the crowd**.

- **Example (Product Reviews & Testimonials):**
    - *"Thousands of 5-star reviews—see why everyone loves it!"*
    - Even if reviews are **fabricated or selectively chosen**, the impression that "everyone loves it" makes people trust the product.

- **Example (Live Sales Counters & Order Pop-Ups):**
    - Online stores show **fake notifications** like *"Mark from Texas just bought this item!"* to create an illusion of high demand.

Social proof **short-circuits skepticism**, making people **more likely to buy without hesitation**.

5. Lifestyle Branding: Selling an Identity, Not a Product

The most successful brands don't just sell products—they **sell a lifestyle and identity**. Consumers don't just buy the item; they buy **who they want to become**.

- **Example (Apple & Luxury Brands):**
    - Apple's ads don't focus on tech specs—they focus on status, creativity, and innovation.
    - People buy iPhones not just for the device, but to signal social status.

- **Example (High-Fashion & Designer Labels):**
    - The **brand itself** becomes the product. A Gucci bag is just a bag—until it is associated with **wealth, power, and exclusivity**.

By linking a product to **identity, success, and social status**, advertisers create **emotional attachment**, making people **feel incomplete without it**.

How to Defend Against Advertising Manipulation

1. Recognize Emotional Triggers in Ads

Whenever you feel an **emotional response** to an ad (fear, excitement, urgency), stop and ask:

- *"Is this a real problem or one that's being manufactured?"*
- *"Am I being pressured to act quickly to avoid missing out?"*

If an ad **makes you feel anxious, insecure, or pressured**, it is likely a **manipulation tactic** rather than genuine value.

2. Question the Scarcity & Exclusivity Tactics

Before making a purchase based on scarcity, ask:

- *"Is this actually rare, or is it just being marketed that way?"*
- *"Would I want this if it wasn't 'limited edition'?"*

Most scarcity tactics **are artificially created** to force urgency. Recognizing this weakens their influence.

3. Separate the Product from the Identity Being Sold

When a brand **sells a lifestyle**, ask:

- *"Do I actually need this, or do I just like the image it portrays?"*
- *"Am I buying this for quality, or just for the status attached to it?"*

Removing **the emotional attachment** allows for **rational decision-making** instead of impulse buying.

Final Thought: Why Consumer Manipulation is So Effective

Advertising is a **psychological war on consumer perception**. The most successful brands **don't just sell products**—they shape desires, create emotional needs, and manipulate perception.

By mastering these tactics, an influencer can:

- **Increase perceived value without changing the actual product.**

- Make people buy based on emotion rather than logic.
- Create urgency and scarcity to force immediate action.

Understanding **how businesses control consumer behavior** is the first step in resisting **unconscious manipulation**—and in learning to use these techniques **ethically** for persuasion and influence.

Politics & Propaganda: Shaping Public Opinion

Politics is not about truth—it is about **perception management**. Governments, political leaders, and media organizations use **psychological manipulation** to control public opinion, steer national conversations, and maintain power.

From **propaganda campaigns to emotional rhetoric, selective framing, and fear-based messaging**, political influence is designed to **bypass rational thinking** and make people follow **ideologies, policies, and leaders** without questioning.

This section reveals the **tactics used to manipulate public perception**, showing how governments, corporations, and interest groups shape narratives to gain power and control.

How Political Manipulation Works: Controlling the Narrative

The human brain is wired to **trust authority figures, seek belonging, and fear uncertainty**. Political manipulation exploits these instincts by:

1. **Reframing reality** – Controlling how information is presented to shift perception.
2. **Appealing to emotions** – Using fear, anger, and hope to override logic.
3. **Using repetition and propaganda** – Making people believe a message simply by repeating it.
4. **Dividing populations** – Creating an "us vs. them" mentality to strengthen loyalty.

By **controlling the flow of information**, political leaders and media outlets can **shape reality** without needing to present actual facts.

Tactics Used to Shape Public Opinion

1. Framing: How the Same Event is Shown in Different Ways

Framing is the technique of **presenting the same facts in a way that influences perception**.

- **Example (News Media Bias):**
  - A news outlet supporting a political leader might say:
    - *"The government is making strong efforts to reduce unemployment."*
  - An opposing outlet might say:
    - *"Despite efforts, unemployment remains high under this administration."*
  - Both statements are factually true, but the framing creates opposite reactions.

- **Example (Political Debates & Spin Tactics):**
  - A politician accused of corruption might **reframe the accusation** by saying:
    - *"This is just a politically motivated attack from my enemies."*
  - This shifts focus away from the allegations and toward defending the leader.

Framing **controls what people focus on**, influencing how they interpret events **without altering the facts**.

2. Fear-Based Messaging: Controlling Through Anxiety

Fear is one of the **most powerful political tools** because a fearful population is **easier to control**.

- **Example (Terrorism & National Security):**
  - Governments justify increased surveillance, military action, or emergency laws by creating fear:
    - *"We must take extreme measures to protect you from threats."*

- o Citizens **accept the loss of privacy and rights** because they believe it keeps them safe.

▸ **Example (Elections & Campaigns):**
- o Politicians use fear to attack opponents:
  - *"If my opponent wins, crime will rise, and the economy will collapse."*
- o Fear-based voting prevents logical policy analysis and makes people vote based on emotional survival instincts.

Fear overrides **critical thinking**, making people **seek protection over freedom**.

3. The Illusion of Choice: Controlling Outcomes No Matter What

Most political systems present voters with **only a few viable options**—but all are pre-selected to maintain control.

▸ **Example (Two-Party Systems):**
- o In many countries, voters are given **two main choices**, but both parties **serve corporate or elite interests**.
- o People **believe they are making a free choice**, but the system **ensures the outcome serves the ruling class**.

▸ **Example (Referendums & Policy Manipulation):**
- o A government gives citizens two options in a public vote, but both options benefit those in power.
- o People feel like they had a say, but the system was rigged from the start.

By **limiting choices**, people **feel in control while unknowingly serving the manipulator's agenda**.

4. Repetition & The Illusion of Truth

When people hear something **enough times**, they start to believe it—**even without evidence**.

▸ **Example (Political Slogans & Messaging):**
- o Politicians repeat simple phrases like:

- "*Make America Great Again*" or "*Yes We Can.*"
    - The brain **accepts the phrase as truth** simply because of repetition.
- **Example (Media Narratives):**
    - News outlets **repeat a claim daily**, even without proof.
    - Over time, people **assume it must be true** because **they've** heard it so often.

The **more often a statement is repeated**, the more it becomes **subconsciously accepted**—regardless of reality.

5. Creating Division: Us vs. Them Mentality

Leaders stay in power by **dividing people** into opposing groups.

- **Example (Racial, Religious, or Ideological Division):**
    - A politician blames social problems on **an external group** (immigrants, the rich, the poor, a different race or religion).
    - People stop questioning **the real issues** and instead fight each other—**allowing the leader to maintain control**.
- **Example (Class & Economic Warfare):**
    - Elites encourage the poor and middle class to fight over economic scraps, so they don't unite against the real power structures.
    - As long as people are fighting each other, they aren't resisting the system.

Dividing populations **prevents unity**—and a **divided society is easier to rule**.

How to Defend Against Political Manipulation

1. Question How Information is Framed

When reading news or political statements, ask:

- *"Is this fact, or just a way of presenting the fact?"*
- *"What is being left out of this narrative?"*

Changing the framing of information often reveals hidden bias.

2. Recognize When Fear is Being Used

Whenever a politician or media outlet pushes fear, stop and ask:

- ▶ *"Is this an actual threat, or is it exaggerated to create panic?"*
- ▶ *"Who benefits from making me afraid?"*

Fear is **a control mechanism**—understanding this **reduces its power over your decisions**.

3. Avoid Emotional Reactivity

When political topics **trigger anger or fear**, pause and ask:

- ▶ *"Am I reacting emotionally, or thinking critically?"*
- ▶ *"Is someone trying to make me feel this way to push an agenda?"*

Emotional manipulation **relies on fast, irrational responses**—slowing down allows logical thinking to take over.

4. Look Beyond Mainstream Choices

If a political system offers **only two or three mainstream options**, consider:

- ▶ *"Are there alternative perspectives being hidden or discredited?"*
- ▶ *"Do all available choices serve the same power structures?"*

Questioning **who benefits from limited choices** often reveals hidden control tactics.

Final Thought: Why Political Manipulation is So Effective

Political control is **not about truth—it is about shaping public perception**. The most successful political systems:

- ▶ **Use framing to control interpretation of events.**
- ▶ **Trigger fear to force compliance.**
- ▶ **Repeat simple messages to bypass logic.**
- ▶ **Create division to prevent unity and resistance.**

By mastering these tactics, an influencer can **steer public opinion, shape beliefs, and maintain long-term power**—without people ever realizing they are being controlled.

Social Media: The Algorithmic Manipulation Machine

Social media is not just a communication tool—it is a **psychological manipulation engine** designed to control **what people see, believe, and engage with**. Unlike traditional media, which had editorial oversight, social media platforms use **AI-driven algorithms** to **steer thoughts, behaviors, and emotions** in ways that benefit advertisers, corporations, and political groups.

From **dopamine-driven engagement loops to censorship, shadow banning, and viral outrage cycles**, this section exposes how social media platforms shape public perception and **control the flow of information**—often without users realizing they are being manipulated.

How Social Media Algorithms Control Thought

Social media platforms are powered by **self-learning AI algorithms** that monitor **everything a user does**—what they like, share, watch, comment on, and even **how long they pause on a post**. This data is then **used to control what they see next**, shaping their worldview.

The key principles behind social media manipulation are:

1. **Engagement is prioritized over truth** – Platforms show **what gets the most reactions**, not what is most accurate.
2. **Echo chambers reinforce existing beliefs** – Users are fed content that aligns with their views, creating **ideological bubbles**.
3. **Negative emotions drive the most engagement** – Fear, outrage, and controversy keep people scrolling.
4. **The algorithm learns to manipulate individual behavior** – AI detects what **triggers each user emotionally** and exploits it.

Social media is **not neutral**—it is an **engineered system** designed to **shape perception, emotion, and action**.

Tactics Used to Manipulate Users on Social Media

1. Dopamine Loops: Addicting Users to Engagement

Social media hijacks the brain's dopamine system—the same system that controls addiction, pleasure, and reward-seeking behavior.

- **Example (Endless Scrolling & Notifications):**
    - Platforms use **infinite scrolling** to keep users **hooked**.
    - Notifications **trigger small dopamine hits**, making people **crave engagement**.
- **Example (Likes, Shares, and Comments):**
    - Social validation **releases dopamine**, making users addicted to **approval and attention**.

These techniques rewire the brain, making people obsessed with engagement and constantly seeking more.

2. Algorithmic Censorship & Shadow Banning

Social media platforms **control which ideas spread** by suppressing content that does not align with their preferred narratives.

- **Example (Political & Social Control):**
    - Certain viewpoints are **buried in search results**, while others are **boosted artificially**.
- **Example (Shadow Banning Tactics):**
    - Users are **not told** their content is restricted—they just receive **less engagement over time**, making them **less likely to post controversial content**.

By **silencing certain perspectives**, platforms create **a controlled reality** where only pre-approved narratives dominate.

3. Outrage Engineering: Triggering Emotional Reactions for Profit

Negative emotions—**anger, fear, and outrage**—generate **more engagement** than neutral or positive emotions. Platforms exploit this by **pushing controversial content** to **increase time spent online**.

- **Example (Political Division & Media Outrage):**
  - Content designed to make users angry is shown more often because it keeps them engaged longer.
- **Example (Culture Wars & Identity Politics):**
  - People are fed divisive content that makes them argue, fight, and share.

Outrage **keeps people emotionally hooked**, preventing them from thinking critically about the content they consume.

4. The Echo Chamber Effect: Reinforcing Existing Beliefs

Social media tracks a user's political, social, and ideological preferences—then feeds them content that reinforces their beliefs.

- **Example (Radicalization & Political Extremes):**
  - Someone who **watches one conspiracy video** is suddenly recommended **dozens more**, making them **fall deeper into the belief system**.
- **Example (News Feed Bias & Ideological Bubbles):**
  - Conservative users see **only conservative content**; liberal users see **only liberal content**.
  - Over time, people **lose the ability to think critically** because they **only see one side of reality**.

Echo chambers prevent exposure to different perspectives, making people easier to manipulate.

5. Manufactured Virality: Controlling Trends and Public Opinion

Not everything that goes viral happens naturally. Platforms and media companies manufacture viral trends to push specific narratives.

- **Example (Political & Social Movements):**
  - Certain hashtags and movements **receive algorithmic boosts**, making them seem **more popular than they actually are**.

- Example (Celebrity & Product Promotion):
  - Influencers are **paid to promote trends**, making them **appear organic** when they are actually **engineered marketing campaigns**.

By **controlling what trends**, social media platforms **shape what people talk about, care about, and believe in**.

How Social Media is Used for Mass Manipulation

1. Psychological Warfare & Political Propaganda

Governments and intelligence agencies **use social media to manipulate populations**.

- Example (Election Influence & Misinformation):
  - Foreign governments **spread false stories** to influence elections.
  - AI-powered bots **create thousands of fake accounts** to push political narratives.

Social media is a **battleground for psychological influence**, where **truth is secondary to control**.

2. Corporate Manipulation & Consumer Control

Companies **buy user data** and use it to **psychologically manipulate consumers** into making **unconscious purchasing decisions**.

- Example (Targeted Advertising & Personalized Persuasion):
  - AI analyzes a user's **habits, fears, and desires**—then **shows ads that exploit those vulnerabilities**.

Users **believe they are making independent choices**, when in reality, their behavior is **being guided by AI-powered marketing systems**.

3. Social Credit Systems & Behavioral Conditioning

Some governments **use social media data** to **punish or reward citizens** based on their online behavior.

- **Example (China's Social Credit System):**
  - The government **tracks online actions**—liking the "wrong" post can lower a citizen's score.
  - Those with **low scores** face **travel restrictions, job loss, and banking penalties.**

By linking **online behavior to real-world consequences**, governments **ensure obedience through digital surveillance.**

How to Defend Against Social Media Manipulation

1. Reduce Algorithmic Influence

Take control of what you see:

- **Turn off personalized recommendations**—manually search for content.
- **Follow diverse sources** to break out of echo chambers.
- **Limit social media exposure** to prevent emotional manipulation.

2. Recognize Engagement Traps

Before reacting to an emotional post, ask:

- *"Am I being triggered to respond emotionally?"*
- *"Is this content designed to divide people?"*

Avoid **participating in outrage cycles**, which only strengthen **algorithmic control** over behavior.

3. Protect Privacy & Avoid Data Exploitation

Since data is used to **manipulate decisions**, protect yourself by:

- **Disabling tracking permissions** on apps.
- **Using encrypted messaging services** to avoid behavioral profiling.
- **Being aware of how personal data is monetized and exploited.**

Final Thought: Social Media as a Digital Mind Control System

Social media is not just about **communication**—it is an **engineered environment** designed to **control emotions, shape opinions, and drive engagement for profit and power.**

By understanding its manipulation tactics, an individual can:

- **Resist algorithmic control and bias.**
- **Avoid emotional and psychological exploitation.**
- **Think independently rather than being shaped by AI-driven influence.**

Mastering these defenses ensures that social media **remains a tool for information, rather than a tool for unconscious mind control.**

Personal Relationships: Subtle Control in Everyday Interactions

Manipulation isn't just used by governments, corporations, and media—it happens in **personal relationships every day**. Whether in **friendships, romantic relationships, family dynamics, or workplaces**, subtle psychological tactics are often used to **gain control, enforce dependency, or steer behavior** without the other person realizing it.

From **gaslighting and guilt-tripping to love bombing and silent treatment**, this section explores the most common forms of everyday manipulation—how to **recognize, resist, and counteract them** before they take control.

How Manipulation Works in Personal Relationships

The human brain is wired to **seek connection, approval, and validation**. Manipulators exploit these instincts by:

1. **Creating emotional highs and lows** – Keeping the target in a cycle of reward and punishment.
2. **Triggering guilt, fear, or obligation** – Making the target feel responsible for the manipulator's happiness.

3. **Controlling information and perception** – Shaping how the target views reality.
4. **Isolating the target** – Removing outside influences that could break the manipulator's control.

Unlike business or political manipulation, **personal manipulation is often emotional rather than logical**, making it more difficult to detect.

Common Manipulation Tactics in Personal Relationships

1. Gaslighting: Making Someone Question Reality

Gaslighting is a form of **psychological control** where the manipulator **denies, twists, or distorts reality**, making the target doubt their memory, perception, or sanity.

- **Example (Romantic Relationships):**
    - A partner repeatedly denies something they said or did:
        - *"I never said that. You must be imagining things."*
    - Over time, the victim **starts questioning their own memory**, making them more dependent on the manipulator for truth.

- **Example (Workplace & Friendships):**
    - A manipulative boss **blames an employee for mistakes they didn't make**, making them feel incompetent and reliant on the boss's approval.

Gaslighting **erodes confidence**, making the victim **easier to control**.

2. Guilt-Tripping: Using Emotional Debt as Leverage

Guilt is a powerful tool for manipulation because it **creates an emotional obligation** to comply with the manipulator's demands.

- Example (Family & Parental Manipulation):
    - A parent might say:
        - *"After all I've done for you, you can't even do this one thing for me?"*
    - This **creates emotional debt**, making the child feel like they must comply.

- Example (Romantic Relationships):
    - A partner pressures the other by saying:
        - *"If you really loved me, you'd do this."*

Guilt-tripping **turns relationships into power imbalances**, where the manipulator **controls through obligation**.

3. Love Bombing: Overwhelming Someone with Affection to Create Dependency

Love bombing is a technique where a manipulator **floods the target with attention, affection, and validation**—only to later use it as **control leverage**.

- **Example (Romantic Manipulation):**
    - In the early stages, a manipulator might say:
        - *"You're the best thing that ever happened to me! I've never felt this way before!"*
    - The target **becomes emotionally addicted** to the intense affection.
    - Later, the manipulator **withdraws affection**, making the target **desperate to earn it back**.
- **Example (Friendships & Social Manipulation):**
    - A new friend **constantly compliments, supports, and includes someone**, only to later **become controlling and demanding**.

Love bombing **creates emotional addiction**, making the victim **easier to manipulate later**.

4. The Silent Treatment: Weaponizing Absence for Control

Instead of direct conflict, some manipulators use **silence and withdrawal** to punish and control others.

- **Example (Romantic & Family Manipulation):**
    - A partner **stops responding, ignores texts, or refuses to speak** after an argument.
    - The target **feels intense emotional distress** and **is forced to apologize or change behavior** to regain connection.

- **Example (Friendships & Social Exclusion):**
  - A group of friends **suddenly ignores someone** as punishment for not conforming.
  - The fear of exclusion **forces compliance** with the group's expectations.

The silent treatment **manipulates through anxiety**—making the victim **work for emotional reconnection**.

5. Passive-Aggression: Controlling Through Subtle Attacks

Passive-aggression allows a manipulator to **criticize, guilt-trip, or undermine someone** while maintaining **plausible deniability**.

- **Example (Workplace & Social Circles):**
  - A co-worker constantly makes **backhanded compliments**:
    - *"Oh wow, I didn't expect you to do such a good job on this."*
  - The target **feels undermined** but struggles to call it out because **it's indirect.**

- **Example (Family & Romantic Relationships):**
  - A manipulative spouse says:
    - *"I guess I'll just do everything myself, since no one ever helps me."*
  - This creates **guilt and pressure** without direct confrontation.

Passive-aggression **creates emotional unease**, making the target **feel guilty or inadequate**.

How to Defend Against Relationship Manipulation

1. Recognize Emotional Manipulation Patterns

Before reacting emotionally, ask:

- *"Am I being guilt-tripped or emotionally blackmailed?"*
- *"Is this person denying things I know to be true?"*

Naming the manipulation **weakens its power** and allows for **rational responses**.

2. Set Boundaries & Stick to Them

Manipulators **push boundaries** to see how much control they can gain. Defend against this by:

- **Clearly stating limits** (e.g., "I will not tolerate being ignored as punishment").
- **Not apologizing for things you didn't do wrong.**
- **Not over-explaining your decisions.**

Enforcing boundaries **prevents emotional dependency**.

3. Resist Emotional Hooks & Pressure

When facing guilt, fear, or love bombing, pause and ask:

- *"Am I being pressured into this decision?"*
- *"Is this person using emotions to manipulate me?"*

A manipulator's power **relies on emotional reactivity**—detaching from the emotions weakens their influence.

4. Create Distance from Toxic Individuals

If manipulation is persistent and harmful:

- **Limit contact** and avoid engaging in their emotional games.
- **Seek external validation** from trusted friends or professionals.
- **Recognize that you do not owe emotional labor to manipulators.**

Distance prevents **further control attempts**.

Final Thought: The Hidden Power Struggles in Personal Relationships

Manipulation in relationships is **subtle but highly effective**. The most successful manipulators:

- **Use gaslighting to rewrite reality.**
- **Exploit guilt and obligation to gain compliance.**
- **Create emotional addiction through love bombing.**
- **Use silent treatment to enforce control.**

By recognizing these tactics, individuals can **defend their emotional autonomy, set strong boundaries, and resist control**—ensuring that their relationships are built on **mutual respect, not manipulation**.

CHAPTER 6
HOW TO DEFEND YOURSELF AGAINST MANIPULATION

Manipulation is most effective when the target **doesn't realize it's happening**. The most skilled manipulators operate **in the shadows**, subtly influencing thoughts, emotions, and behaviors without triggering resistance.

This chapter focuses on **recognizing and neutralizing covert influence tactics**. Whether in business, relationships, politics, or everyday interactions, understanding **how manipulation works** is the first step in preventing **your thoughts and decisions from being controlled by someone else**.

By mastering **awareness, psychological resilience, and counter-manipulation strategies**, you can ensure that you remain in control of your own **mind, emotions, and choices**.

Recognizing Covert Influence: The Hidden Red Flags

The first step in defending against manipulation is **learning to recognize it in real-time**. While some forms of control are **obvious**, most manipulative tactics are **subtle and disguised as normal interactions**.

This section breaks down **the psychological red flags of covert influence**, helping you identify when someone is **guiding your thoughts, emotions, and behaviors without your awareness**.

The Hidden Signs of Manipulation

Manipulation is **not about forcing someone to act**—it's about **shaping perception so that the target believes they are acting on their own free will**. The following red flags indicate that someone may be subtly exerting control over you.

1. Sudden Emotional Reactions That Feel Out of Character

One of the strongest indicators of covert influence is when you **suddenly feel extreme emotions**—anger, guilt, fear, or urgency—without fully understanding why.

- **Example (Sales & Negotiation Manipulation):**
  - A salesperson creates **artificial urgency**:
    - *"This deal expires in 10 minutes! You don't want to miss out, do you?"*
  - You feel pressured and **rush into a decision**, only to regret it later.

- **Example (Relationship Manipulation):**
  - A friend or partner triggers guilt:
    - *"You never support me the way I support you."*
  - You suddenly feel obligated to do something you wouldn't normally do.

Red Flag: If an interaction **suddenly makes you feel anxious, guilty, or pressured**, pause and ask:

- *"Why am I feeling this way?"*
- *"Is someone deliberately trying to make me react emotionally?"*

Manipulators **exploit emotions to bypass logical thinking**—recognizing this gives you **control over your reactions**.

2. When a Person's Words and Actions Don't Match

Manipulators often say one thing while **doing another**, creating confusion that makes them **hard to pin down**.

- **Example (Workplace & Social Manipulation):**
  - A co-worker tells you they support your promotion, but **spreads subtle doubts about your abilities** to others behind your back.

- **Example (Romantic Manipulation):**
  - A partner claims: *"I love you,"* but **constantly ignores or belittles you.**

Red Flag: If someone's words **don't align with their actions**, they may be using **manipulation to disguise their true intentions**.

To counter this, trust patterns of behavior over spoken assurances.

3. Shifting Blame & Avoiding Responsibility

A classic sign of manipulation is **never admitting fault**—instead, manipulators **redirect blame onto others.**

- **Example (Gaslighting in Relationships):**
    - You confront someone for breaking a promise, and they respond:
        - *"You're too sensitive. It's not a big deal."*
    - Instead of taking responsibility, they **make you question your own reaction.**

- **Example (Political & Corporate Manipulation):**
    - A leader blames **external factors** for failure:
        - *"The economy is bad because of the other party's policies."*
    - This deflects **responsibility**, keeping the manipulator in power.

Red Flag: If someone **always shifts blame onto others**, they are likely using **manipulation to avoid accountability.**

4. Creating Confusion & Mental Exhaustion

Manipulators **overwhelm targets with conflicting information**, making them too mentally exhausted to resist.

- **Example (Workplace Power Moves):**
    - A boss keeps **changing project deadlines**, making employees **too confused and exhausted to push back against unfair treatment.**

- **Example (Toxic Relationships & Social Manipulation):**
    - A partner **sends mixed signals**, alternating between **affection and emotional withdrawal**, keeping the target **off-balance and desperate for approval.**

Red Flag: If you feel **mentally drained after interactions** with someone, they may be using **confusion as a manipulation tool**.

To counter this, step back and **analyze patterns rather than reacting emotionally to each situation**.

5. Using "Favor Banking" to Create Debt-Based Control

Some manipulators **deliberately do favors** so they can later **demand something in return**.

- **Example (Corporate & Business Influence):**
    - A powerful executive **mentors a younger employee**, only to later say:
        - *"You owe me. I expect full loyalty."*
- **Example (Friendships & Social Control):**
    - A friend **constantly gives gifts or does favors**, but later uses this as leverage:
        - *"I've done so much for you—how can you say no to me now?"*

Red Flag: If someone's generosity **feels transactional**, they may be **building a sense of debt to control future behavior**.

To counter this, recognize that **true kindness has no strings attached**—you are **not obligated to repay manipulative favors**.

6. Extreme Reactions When You Set Boundaries

A major red flag is when **someone becomes angry, distant, or manipulative** the moment you **assert your independence**.

- **Example (Toxic Relationships):**
    - You say: *"I need some space."*
    - They react with **anger, silent treatment, or guilt-tripping** to make you **backtrack on your decision**.
- **Example (Workplace Power Games):**
    - You decline extra work, and your boss implies you are **not a team player** to make you comply.

Red Flag: If someone **can't handle you setting boundaries**, they likely benefit from keeping you under their influence.

To defend yourself, stand firm—**healthy people respect personal limits**.

How to Respond to Covert Influence

1. Slow Down & Avoid Emotional Reactions

Manipulation relies on **making you react instantly**. By **delaying your response**, you regain **mental control**.

- Instead of answering immediately, say:
    - "I need time to think about this."
- If you feel **emotionally triggered**, pause and ask:
    - "Am I being manipulated into feeling this way?"

Slowing down prevents impulse-driven compliance.

2. Ask Clarifying Questions

Manipulation often **falls apart under scrutiny**. To expose it, ask:

- *"Can you explain why this is urgent?"*
- *"Are you saying this because it benefits me or you?"*

Forcing a manipulator to **clarify their logic** weakens their influence.

3. Set Clear, Non-Negotiable Boundaries

The best defense against manipulation is **being firm in what you accept and reject**.

- If someone **pressures you**, say:
    - *"I've made my decision, and I'm not changing it."*
- If someone **plays emotional games**, respond with:
    - *"I don't engage in guilt-tripping. If you respect me, you'll respect my choices."*

Clear boundaries **deter further manipulation attempts**.

Final Thought: Protecting Your Mental & Emotional Autonomy

The most dangerous form of manipulation is **the kind that goes unnoticed**. The most skilled manipulators:

- Create emotional triggers to override logical thinking.
- Use blame-shifting and confusion to avoid accountability.
- Manipulate generosity and obligation to gain long-term control.

By **learning to recognize the red flags**, you ensure that **your decisions remain your own**—not shaped by hidden influence tactics.

Becoming "Unmanipulatable": Strengthening Psychological Resistance

The key to **resisting manipulation** is developing **psychological resilience**. Skilled manipulators exploit **emotional triggers, cognitive biases, and subconscious patterns**, but once you strengthen your **mental defenses**, their influence loses its power.

This section explores the **core strategies for making yourself unmanipulatable**—building self-awareness, emotional stability, and critical thinking skills to ensure that **no one can control your thoughts, emotions, or decisions**.

The Foundation of Psychological Resistance

Manipulation works because people:

1. **Seek approval and social validation.**
2. **Fear missing out, loss, or conflict.**
3. **Rely on emotions over logic in decision-making.**

By reversing these tendencies and developing **self-sufficiency, critical awareness, and emotional discipline**, you become significantly **harder to manipulate**.

The following strategies help **neutralize psychological control tactics**.

1. Master Emotional Detachment: Recognizing When Emotions Are Being Weaponized

Manipulators **trigger emotions** because emotions override **rational thinking**. If you can **detach from emotional reactions**, you prevent external influence.

- **Example (Sales & Marketing Influence):**
    - A salesman says:
        - *"This is a once-in-a-lifetime deal!"*
    - Instead of reacting to **fear of missing out (FOMO)**, an emotionally disciplined person pauses, **reflects, and makes a rational choice**.
- **Example (Relationship Manipulation & Guilt-Tripping):**
    - A manipulative partner says:
        - *"If you loved me, you would do this for me."*
    - Instead of giving in to **emotional pressure**, an independent thinker **analyzes the request logically**.

How to Apply This Strategy:

- When you feel a **strong emotional reaction**, ask:
    - *"Is this emotion natural, or is it being manipulated?"*
- Train yourself to **pause before responding**, especially in high-pressure situations.
- Develop **emotional awareness** so you can identify **when someone is trying to hijack your feelings**.

By controlling **your emotions**, you prevent **external forces from controlling you**.

2. Stop Seeking Validation: Building Inner Confidence

One of the biggest reasons people fall for manipulation is **seeking approval and external validation**. When you no longer need **constant reassurance from others**, you become far less **susceptible to influence**.

- **Example (Social & Workplace Manipulation):**
  - A manipulative boss says:
    - *"The team is counting on you—you don't want to let them down, do you?"*
  - A self-secure individual replies:
    - *"I'm happy to contribute, but I make decisions based on my own priorities."*

- **Example (Friendship & Peer Pressure):**
  - A friend pressures you to **do something you're uncomfortable with**, saying:
    - *"Everyone else is doing it—don't be boring."*
  - A strong-minded person responds:
    - *"I don't need to follow the group to be confident in my choices."*

How to Apply This Strategy:

- **Ask yourself**: "Am I making this choice because I want to, or because I want approval?"
- Train yourself to **be comfortable with disapproval**—not everyone's opinion matters.
- Recognize that **manipulators use validation as a weapon**—true confidence is built internally.

When you **stop relying on external approval**, manipulators **lose control over you**.

3. Strengthen Critical Thinking: Questioning Everything You're Told

Manipulators **exploit assumptions, biases, and social conditioning** to shape perceptions. If you automatically **question narratives, motives, and framing**, you become difficult to deceive.

- **Example (Media & Political Manipulation):**
  - A news outlet says:
    - *"Experts agree this is the only logical solution."*

- o A critical thinker asks:
  - ▪ *"Who are these experts? Who benefits from this narrative?"*
- ▶ **Example (Personal Influence & Persuasion):**
  - o A manipulator says:
    - ▪ *"If you don't do this, bad things will happen."*
  - o A critical thinker asks:
    - ▪ *"Is there actual proof, or is this just fear-based manipulation?"*

How to Apply This Strategy:

- ▶ Always ask: "Who benefits if I believe this?"
- ▶ Look for **alternative perspectives** before making decisions.
- ▶ Separate **facts from emotional persuasion**—manipulation thrives on **distorted framing**.

By strengthening **logical thinking**, you prevent others from **controlling your perception of reality**.

4. Set Hard Boundaries: Training People to Respect Your Limits

Manipulators push **boundaries** to test **how much control they can gain**. When you set **clear, firm limits**, it stops control tactics before they begin.

- ▶ **Example (Workplace & Social Pressure):**
  - o A boss expects you to work overtime without pay.
  - o Instead of **giving in**, you say:
    - ▪ *"I don't work unpaid hours. If this is necessary, we need to discuss compensation."*
- ▶ **Example (Toxic Relationships & Emotional Games):**
  - o A friend constantly asks for favors but never reciprocates.
  - o Instead of complying, you say:
    - ▪ *"I'm happy to help sometimes, but I expect balance in friendships."*

How to Apply This Strategy:

- Be clear: **"This is my limit, and I won't compromise."**
- Enforce consequences: **If someone repeatedly pushes a boundary, distance yourself.**
- Recognize that **people who don't respect boundaries are testing how much control they can have over you**.

Strong boundaries signal **you cannot be easily manipulated.**

5. Control Your Information: Stop Giving Manipulators Leverage

Manipulators **collect personal details, fears, and insecurities**—then use them as leverage later. By **limiting what you reveal**, you **reduce their ability to control you**.

- **Example (Workplace & Professional Boundaries):**
    - A co-worker **asks personal questions** to find weaknesses.
    - Instead of oversharing, you keep responses **neutral and professional**.
- **Example (Toxic Relationships & Emotional Blackmail):**
    - A manipulative person **demands personal details**, then later uses them against you.
    - Instead of exposing vulnerabilities, you share **only what is necessary**.

How to Apply This Strategy:

- Limit how much personal information you share with **people you don't fully trust**.
- If someone **asks invasive questions**, redirect the conversation or set a boundary.
- Remember: **Information is power**—control what you reveal, and you control how much leverage others have over you.

Final Thought: Becoming Immune to Psychological Manipulation

To become truly **unmanipulatable**, you must:

- **Detach from emotional manipulation** – Recognize when emotions are being used to control decisions.
- **Stop seeking validation** – Be confident in yourself without needing approval from others.
- **Strengthen critical thinking** – Always question motives, narratives, and hidden agendas.
- **Set clear boundaries** – Make it known what you will and won't accept.
- **Control your information** – Limit what others know about you to prevent leverage.

Once you develop **psychological resistance**, manipulators **lose their ability to control you**—and you become the one who dictates your own thoughts, actions, and reality.

The Mental Autonomy Blueprint: Staying in Control of Your Own Mind

The final step in defending against manipulation is achieving **mental autonomy**—the ability to think independently, make decisions based on logic rather than emotion, and resist external control.

This section presents **a systematic approach to maintaining mental independence**, ensuring that no manipulator—whether in personal relationships, business, politics, or media—can steer your mind without your awareness.

Why Mental Autonomy Matters: The Battle for Your Mind

Most people believe they are **in control of their own thoughts and decisions**, but **external forces constantly shape perception**. Governments, corporations, media, and individuals use **psychological manipulation** to **guide beliefs and behaviors** without triggering resistance.

To break free from manipulation, you must develop:

1. **Emotional detachment** – The ability to recognize and regulate emotional triggers.
2. **Cognitive independence** – The habit of questioning narratives and making logical assessments.
3. **Information control** – The skill of filtering and verifying what enters your mind.

Mastering these areas makes you **resistant to external influence**, giving you full control over **your own thoughts, choices, and reality**.

1. Emotional Mastery: Preventing Emotional Hijacking

Manipulators exploit emotions—especially **fear, guilt, excitement, and anger**—to override logical thinking. To maintain **mental autonomy**, you must learn to **regulate emotional responses**.

How to Apply Emotional Mastery:

-
- **Pause Before Reacting** – If a situation triggers strong emotions, ask:
    - *"Am I reacting instinctively, or am I thinking critically?"*
    - *"Is someone trying to make me feel this way?"*
- **Detach From Fear-Based Messaging** – Recognize when **fear is being used as a control tactic** in sales, politics, or relationships.
- **Practice Emotional Distance** – When faced with pressure, say:
    - *"I'll think about this and get back to you."*
    - This disrupts **impulse-based manipulation** and allows time for logical evaluation.

Once you control **your emotional responses**, you prevent **others from using them against you.**

2. Cognitive Independence: Thinking for Yourself, Not How Others Want You to Think

Manipulators rely on **blind acceptance** of ideas. If you **automatically question narratives, challenge framing, and analyze motives**, you become extremely difficult to manipulate.

How to Develop Cognitive Independence:

- **Always Ask: "Who Benefits?"** – When presented with an idea, consider:
  - *"Who gains if I believe this?"*
  - *"Is this fact, or is it being framed to create a specific reaction?"*
- **Recognize Loaded Language & Emotional Framing** – Be skeptical when words like *"urgent,"* *"everyone agrees,"* or *"this is the only solution"* are used.
- **Seek Contradictory Information** – Challenge your own beliefs by **deliberately exposing yourself to different perspectives**.

By making **critical thinking a habit**, you take back control over **your own perception of reality**.

3. Information Control: Filtering What Enters Your Mind

In today's world, **information overload** is one of the biggest manipulation tools. The more **unfiltered content you consume**, the easier it is for external forces to **shape your thoughts**.

How to Filter & Verify Information:

- **Limit Exposure to Algorithmic Feeds** – Social media and news algorithms **manipulate what you see**. Instead, seek information **manually**.
- **Cross-Check Sources** – Never trust **one version of a story**—look for alternative perspectives.
- **Be Wary of Emotional Triggers in Media** – If a headline makes you **angry, fearful, or outraged**, ask:
  - *"Is this a rational response, or am I being manipulated?"*

Taking control over **your information intake** prevents external forces from **controlling your beliefs**.

4. Personal Boundaries: Controlling Who Influences You

The people you surround yourself with have **a massive impact on your thinking and behavior**. Manipulative individuals often enter personal, social, or professional spaces to **subtly shape your decisions**.

How to Enforce Mental Boundaries:

- **Identify Negative Influences** – If someone **consistently pressures, guilt-trips, or emotionally manipulates** you, create distance.
- **Surround Yourself with Critical Thinkers** – Engage with people who **challenge perspectives rather than enforce conformity**.
- **Limit Personal Information Sharing** – The less **manipulators know about your fears, insecurities, and emotional triggers**, the less power they have over you.

Controlling **who has access to your thoughts and emotions** is key to maintaining **mental independence**.

5. Strategic Non-Reactivity: Controlling How Others Perceive Your Responses

One of the most **powerful defense mechanisms against manipulation** is becoming **strategically non-reactive**—choosing when and how to respond rather than reacting instinctively.

How to Master Non-Reactivity:

- **Delay Responses to Pressure Tactics** – If someone pushes for an immediate reaction, say:
    - *"I need time to think about this."*
    - This forces **manipulators to lose momentum**.
- **Avoid Justifying or Over-Explaining Yourself** – Defending your choices often gives manipulators **more leverage to argue against them**.
- **Control Body Language & Tone** – Stay **calm, composed, and neutral**, even if someone tries to provoke emotional reactions.

By becoming **unpredictable in your reactions**, you **disrupt manipulation attempts** before they can take hold.

6. Mental Reset: Reclaiming Control After Being Manipulated

Even with strong defenses, **everyone is manipulated at some point**. The key is learning how to **reset and recover control quickly**.

How to Reverse Manipulation:

- **Step Back & Analyze the Situation** – Ask:
    - *"What emotion did they use to influence me?"*
    - *"Was I pressured into a decision?"*
- **Reframe the Experience as a Lesson** – Rather than feeling manipulated, view it as a **learning opportunity to strengthen future resistance**.
- **Reassert Boundaries Immediately** – If someone has taken advantage, clarify that **it won't happen again**.

The ability to **identify, correct, and learn from manipulation** ensures long-term **mental autonomy**.

Final Thought: Achieving Full Mental Autonomy

Becoming **immune to manipulation** doesn't mean ignoring influence—it means learning to **control what influences you**. By mastering:

- **Emotional discipline** – Not allowing emotions to override logic.
- **Critical thinking** – Questioning motives, narratives, and framing.
- **Information control** – Filtering and verifying what enters your mind.
- **Personal boundaries** – Limiting the power of external forces.
- **Strategic non-reactivity** – Controlling how others perceive your responses.

You ensure that **every decision you make is your own**—not shaped by hidden forces.

Mental autonomy is the ultimate **shield against manipulation**, ensuring that you remain **in control of your thoughts, choices, and future**.

CHAPTER 7
THE 7-DAY INFLUENCE EXPERIMENT

Understanding manipulation is one thing—applying it is another. This chapter is a **practical challenge**, designed to help you **develop real-world influence skills** by applying the techniques discussed in this book.

For seven days, you will **test persuasion, psychological triggers, and covert influence techniques** in everyday situations. Each exercise builds upon the last, allowing you to **observe manipulation in action and refine your ability to influence others**.

By the end of this experiment, you will:

- Recognize manipulation instantly in any interaction.
- Gain confidence in using persuasion techniques ethically.
- Sharpen your ability to influence without detection.

Day 1-2: Practicing Subtle Suggestion

The first step in mastering influence is **learning how to plant ideas in someone's mind without them realizing it**.

For these two days, your focus will be on using **subtle suggestion**—a technique that leverages indirect language, repetition, and subconscious priming to make people believe an idea was their own.

How Subtle Suggestion Works

The brain is wired to **process information passively**. When you suggest something in a **non-direct way**, people often internalize it as if it were their own thought.

This is because:

1. **People resist direct commands** – They don't like being told what to do.
2. **Subconscious repetition makes ideas feel familiar** – The brain trusts repeated information.
3. **Framing affects perception** – The way something is presented changes how it's received.

Your goal for Day 1 and Day 2 is to **test these principles in everyday interactions**.

Exercise 1: The "I Wonder" Technique

Instead of telling someone what to do, **frame it as a passing thought or curiosity**.

- **Example (Getting Someone to Pick a Restaurant):**
    - Instead of saying:
        - *"Let's eat at this place."*
    - Say:
        - *"I wonder if that new sushi place is any good…"*
    - If repeated casually, the other person is **more likely to suggest it later** as if it was their idea.

- **Example (Influencing a Decision at Work):**
    - Instead of saying:
        - *"We should try a new strategy."*
    - Say:
        - *"I was just thinking… wouldn't it be interesting to test a new approach?"*

Your Task:

Try using **the "I wonder" technique at least five times** today to see how often people respond as if the idea was theirs.

Exercise 2: Strategic Repetition & Priming

Repetition makes ideas **seem more credible** and **more likely to stick**. Subtle priming works by **introducing an idea multiple times in different ways**.

- Example (Making Someone Think About Travel):
    - Mention a past trip you took.

- Later, comment on a travel-related post on social media.
- A few hours later, say:
  - *"It feels like a great time for a vacation."*
- Over time, this **primes the person's mind toward thinking about travel**—they may even bring it up themselves.

▶ Example (Influencing a Friend's Buying Decision):
- Casually mention a product you're interested in.
- Later, talk about a review or an influencer using it.
- Next time you're together, show them an ad for it.
- By now, they will feel like **buying the product is their own idea**.

Your Task:

Choose a **theme (a product, a place, an action)** and prime someone in your circle by mentioning it **three different ways throughout the day**. Observe if they bring it up later.

Exercise 3: The "Assumed Agreement" Trick

Instead of asking if someone agrees, **talk as if they already do**. This removes hesitation and makes compliance feel natural.

▶ **Example (Getting a Friend to Join You Somewhere):**
- Instead of:
  - *"Do you want to go to the gym later?"*
- Say:
  - *"Since we're both hitting the gym later, what time works best?"*

▶ **Example (Closing a Sale or Negotiation):**
- Instead of:
  - *"Would you like to move forward with this deal?"*
- Say:
  - *"Should we finalize the paperwork today or tomorrow?"*

Your Task:

Use **assumed agreement three times** today and note how people react differently than if you had asked for permission.

Observation & Reflection

At the end of Day 2, ask yourself:

- *Did people respond differently when I used subtle suggestion instead of direct commands?*
- *Which techniques worked best?*
- *Did anyone later suggest something I had subtly planted earlier?*

By observing these effects in action, you will start seeing **how influence works beneath the surface**—a skill you will refine in the next five days.

What's Next?

On **Day 3-4**, you will learn **how to use mirroring and priming to increase influence in conversations**—deepening your ability to build trust and guide interactions without force.

Day 3-4: Building Trust and Influence with Mirroring & Priming

Now that you've practiced **subtle suggestion and priming**, it's time to move to **deeper psychological influence techniques: mirroring and priming for trust-building**.

Mirroring is one of the **fastest ways to create subconscious rapport** with anyone, making them more likely to **trust, like, and agree with you**. Combined with **priming**, this technique allows you to subtly guide conversations and interactions toward your desired outcome.

For the next two days, your goal is to **test these techniques in real interactions** and observe how they **change the way people respond to you**.

1. The Power of Mirroring: Why People Trust Those Who Reflect Them

Mirroring is a **nonverbal influence tactic** where you subtly **copy someone's body language, speech patterns, or energy level** to make them feel connected to you.

This works because:

- People feel comfortable with those who seem like them.
- The brain interprets similarity as trustworthiness.
- Mirroring activates the subconscious need for social bonding.

Your task for **Day 3** is to **apply mirroring in conversations** and observe how it shifts interactions.

Exercise 1: Mirroring Body Language

When talking to someone, subtly **match their posture, hand gestures, or facial expressions**.

- Example (Building Rapport in Social Settings):
    o If someone **leans forward**, slowly do the same.
    o If they **cross their arms**, wait a few seconds, then subtly copy.
    o If they **nod while speaking**, mirror their nodding pattern.

- Example (Workplace or Business Influence):
    o If a colleague **rests their chin on their hand**, do the same after a short delay.
    o If a boss **speaks in a calm, slow tone**, adjust your own tone to match.

Your Task:

Mirror **three different people** today and observe:

- Do they **open up more** in conversation?
- Do they seem **more engaged or trusting**?

Exercise 2: Mirroring Speech Patterns & Tone

People naturally **connect with others who match their vocal style, tone, and pace**. By adjusting your **voice to match the energy of the person you're speaking with**, you create **instant subconscious trust**.

- **Example (Casual Conversations & Friendships):**
    - If someone **speaks fast and energetically**, increase your **speed and enthusiasm** slightly.
    - If they **speak softly and slowly**, lower your own tone and pace.
- **Example (Professional Influence & Negotiation):**
    - If a client **uses formal language**, match their structured style.
    - If they **speak in casual, relaxed phrases**, adjust your speech to be more conversational.

Your Task:

Mirror **three people's vocal style and pace** today and observe:

- Do they **seem more engaged?**
- Do they **respond with more warmth or openness?**

2. Priming: Pre-Framing People's Thoughts Before a Conversation

Priming is a **subconscious influence technique** where you introduce an idea **before** discussing it, making the person more likely to **accept it later**.

Priming works because:

- The brain tends to continue patterns it has already started.
- A concept that has been introduced subtly feels more "natural" when brought up later.
- People often mistake primed ideas as their own thoughts.

Your task for **Day 4** is to **test priming techniques in conversation**.

Exercise 3: Using Priming in Everyday Interactions

Step 1: Introduce a Concept Indirectly

- Mention a **word, theme, or topic casually** at the beginning of a conversation.
- Don't make it obvious—just plant the seed.

Step 2: Reintroduce It Later as a Discussion Point

When you bring it up again, **the person will be more receptive** without realizing why.

- **Example (Social Priming – Steering Conversations):**
    - Early in the day, say:
        - *"I read something interesting about meditation."*
    - Later, when talking about stress, say:
        - *"Have you ever tried meditation? I heard it works well for focus."*
    - Because the idea was **already in their mind**, they will feel **more open to it**.

- **Example (Professional Influence – Subconscious Buy-In):**
    - Early in a meeting, say:
        - *"I've been thinking about ways to improve efficiency."*
    - Later, when presenting a solution, say:
        - *"Since we're all looking for better efficiency, here's an approach that could work."*
    - The **repetition makes the idea seem natural**, increasing the likelihood of agreement.

Your Task:

Use **priming three times** today and observe:

- Do people seem more **receptive when the idea is brought up again?**
- Do they **agree more quickly than usual?**

Observation & Reflection

At the end of Day 4, ask yourself:

- ▸ *Did mirroring change how people interacted with me?*
- ▸ *Did priming make people more receptive to ideas?*
- ▸ *Did these techniques feel natural, or did I need to adjust?*

By observing these techniques **in action**, you will start seeing how **subtle influence works beneath the surface**—giving you a deeper understanding of **covert persuasion skills**.

What's Next?

On **Day 5-6**, you will learn how to use **anchoring and emotional triggers** to create deep subconscious influence—allowing you to shape how people feel about situations, experiences, and even yourself.

Day 5-6: Anchoring & Emotional Triggers in Action

Now that you've practiced **mirroring and priming**, it's time to explore **anchoring and emotional triggers**—two of the most powerful techniques for shaping someone's subconscious perceptions and influencing how they react to you.

Anchoring allows you to **attach a specific feeling or reaction to a word, gesture, or situation**, while emotional triggers **activate deep responses** that override logical thinking.

For the next two days, your goal is to **test these techniques in real interactions** and observe how they **shift people's moods, behaviors, and decisions**.

1. The Power of Anchoring: Creating Subconscious Associations

Anchoring is a **psychological conditioning technique** where you **link a specific stimulus (word, gesture, or tone) with a desired emotional response**. Over time, the target **subconsciously connects the stimulus with that emotion**.

This is used in:

- **Sales & Persuasion** – Creating positive associations with a product or person.
- **Dating & Social Influence** – Linking your presence with good feelings.
- **Leadership & Authority** – Making people feel trust and respect when you speak.

Your task for **Day 5** is to **apply anchoring in conversations** and observe how it influences reactions.

Exercise 1: Using Positive Anchors

The goal is to **attach good emotions to your presence, voice, or gestures** so that people unconsciously feel positive when they interact with you.

Step 1: Choose Your Anchor

- A **specific phrase** (e.g., "That's what I love about you.")
- A **touch or gesture** (e.g., a light touch on the arm when someone laughs)
- A **tone of voice** (e.g., an enthusiastic, warm tone when greeting someone)

Step 2: Pair It with a Positive Emotion

Each time the person **feels good**, repeat the chosen anchor:

- When someone **laughs**, lightly touch their arm or shoulder.
- When they feel **proud of something**, say: *"That's exactly why you're so great at this."*
- When they feel **happy or excited**, match their energy and repeat your anchor phrase.

Over time, their **brain will link that feeling with your presence or words**, making them **feel good around you without knowing why**.

Example Applications:

- **Social Settings:** Attach an anchor to moments of laughter to make people associate fun with you.

- **Business & Leadership:** Use a confident phrase when reinforcing someone's achievements to make them associate motivation with your presence.
- **Romantic Influence:** Pair a subtle touch with moments of closeness so the person feels warmth when you do it later.

Your Task:

Use a positive anchor three times today and observe:

- Does the person **respond more positively** to you over time?
- Do they seem to **engage more or mirror your energy?**

Exercise 2: Breaking Negative Anchors

Sometimes, people **accidentally associate you with stress or discomfort**. Breaking negative anchors ensures that **your presence isn't linked to tension**.

Step 1: Identify Negative Patterns

- Does someone **always seem tense when you approach?**
- Does a co-worker **look irritated when you start a conversation?**
- Does a friend **associate you with stressful topics?**

Step 2: Disrupt the Pattern

- Change the **setting or tone** before serious discussions.
- Start with a **positive or unrelated topic** before addressing difficult issues.
- Introduce a **humor break** if someone associates you with tension.

Your Task:

Find **one situation** where someone reacts negatively to you and **reframe their perception using a positive anchor.**

2. Emotional Triggers: Activating Deep Psychological Responses

Certain emotions **override logical thinking**, making people **more suggestible and responsive**. The key to influence is knowing **which emotions to trigger and when**.

Common **manipulators of emotional responses** include:

- **Excitement & Enthusiasm** – Increases agreement and buy-in.
- **Urgency & Scarcity** – Triggers immediate action.
- **Nostalgia & Sentimentality** – Makes people more open and trusting.
- **Fear & Uncertainty** – Creates compliance (but should be used ethically).

Your task for **Day 6** is to test **emotional triggers in conversation** and observe their effects.

Exercise 3: Triggering Excitement & Enthusiasm

When people are excited, they **agree more easily, commit to ideas faster, and associate you with positive experiences**.

How to Trigger Excitement:

- **Match or exceed their energy level.**
- **Use vivid, engaging storytelling.**
- **Focus on possibilities and benefits rather than negatives.**

Example Applications:

- Social Influence:
    - Instead of saying, *"We should check out this place,"*
    - Say: *"This spot has the best energy! Imagine the music, the crowd—let's make a night out of it!"*

- Sales & Persuasion:
    - Instead of saying, *"This could work for you,"*
    - Say: *"Imagine how much easier your life will be with this—it's a total game-changer."*

Your Task:

Test **three instances of enthusiasm mirroring** today and observe:

- Do people **respond more positively** to your suggestions?
- Do they **agree faster than usual?**

Exercise 4: Creating Urgency & Scarcity Without Pressure

Urgency increases **decision-making speed**. Instead of **forcing** urgency, introduce it **naturally**.

How to Introduce Urgency:

- Casually mention limited opportunities.
- Use time-sensitive wording without pressure.
- Let people feel they're making the choice on their own.

Example Applications:

- **Encouraging Action in Business:**
  - *"This strategy has worked for a lot of people, but the market is shifting—those who move fast get ahead."*

- **Social or Relationship Influence:**
  - *"We have to experience this together soon—things like this don't come around often!"*

Your Task:

Use two **urgency-based phrases** today and observe:

- Do people act **more quickly?**
- Do they seem **more committed** to decisions?

Observation & Reflection

At the end of Day 6, ask yourself:

- *Did people seem to respond to my presence differently when I used anchoring?*
- *Did emotional triggers increase their enthusiasm or urgency?*
- *Were people making decisions faster or responding more positively?*

By refining these techniques, you will learn how **subconscious associations shape behavior**, allowing you to **steer conversations, emotions, and interactions with ease.**

What's Next?

On **Day 7**, you will bring everything together—testing **a full set of influence techniques in a real conversation, sale, or negotiation**.

Day 7: Testing Full Influence Techniques in a Real Situation

Now that you've practiced **subtle suggestion, mirroring, priming, anchoring, and emotional triggers**, it's time for the **final challenge**—using all of these techniques together in a real-world situation.

Today, your goal is to **apply multiple influence strategies in a single conversation, sale, negotiation, or social interaction** and observe how effectively you can **steer the outcome in your favor**.

Step 1: Choose Your Test Situation

Pick a real-life scenario where you can **apply influence techniques naturally**. Some ideas include:

- **Social Setting:** Convince a group to choose your suggested activity or restaurant.
- **Workplace Interaction:** Guide a meeting or discussion in your preferred direction.
- **Sales or Negotiation:** Persuade someone to agree to a deal or decision.
- **Personal Relationship:** Get someone to see a situation from your perspective.

Once you've chosen the situation, plan how you will apply **at least three influence techniques**.

Step 2: Structure the Conversation Using Influence Techniques

Use the following structure to **steer the interaction subtly**.

1. Start with Priming

Before making your main suggestion, **introduce key themes or ideas subtly** so they feel familiar later.

- **Example (Social Setting – Choosing a Restaurant):**
    - Earlier in the day, mention: *"I've been craving sushi lately."*
    - Later, casually ask: *"Have you ever tried that new sushi spot? I heard it's great."*

- **Example (Workplace – Guiding a Decision):**
    - Early in the meeting, say: *"A lot of successful teams are shifting toward this approach."*
    - Later, present your idea framed as a **natural progression** of that thought.

2. Build Rapport with Mirroring & Matching

During the conversation, **subtly match the other person's tone, pace, and gestures** to increase trust.

- If they **lean forward**, do the same after a few seconds.
- If they **speak quickly and energetically**, slightly increase your energy level.
- If they **use certain phrases frequently**, incorporate them into your speech.

This makes them feel **more connected to you subconsciously**, making them **more likely to agree**.

3. Use Anchoring to Reinforce Positive Emotions

Throughout the interaction, **attach good feelings to your presence and ideas**.

- If the person laughs or reacts positively, **lightly touch their arm or nod in agreement** (this associates good emotions with your presence).
- Use **a specific phrase repeatedly** during moments of positivity (e.g., *"That's exactly the kind of thinking I admire."*).
- Frame your suggestion **in a way that recalls positive moments** (e.g., *"Remember how much fun we had last time? This will be just like that."*).

Over time, they will **link your idea to good feelings**, making them more likely to accept it.

4. Introduce Emotional Triggers to Strengthen Persuasion

Use **subtle emotional appeals** to create a sense of **urgency, exclusivity, or excitement**.

- ▶ Example (Sales or Business Setting – Creating Urgency):
    - o *"The best opportunities don't stay open for long, and I want you to be ahead of the curve."*
- ▶ Example (Personal Influence – Creating Excitement):
    - o *"Imagine how amazing it'll feel once we do this—it's going to be an experience we'll never forget."*
- ▶ Example (Group Decision – Using Social Proof):
    - o *"A lot of people I trust have already tried this, and they loved it."*

When **people feel emotionally engaged**, they are **far more likely to say yes**.

5. Close the Influence Loop with the Assumed Agreement Technique

Instead of asking for agreement directly, **frame it as a given**.

- ▶ Example (Convincing a Friend to Try Something New):
    - o Instead of: *"Do you want to go?"*
    - o Say: *"So what time should we go?"*
- ▶ Example (Closing a Business Deal):
    - o Instead of: *"Would you like to move forward?"*
    - o Say: *"Let's finalize the details so we can get started."*

This removes hesitation and makes **compliance feel like the natural next step**.

Step 3: Observe the Results & Adjust

As you go through the conversation, pay attention to:

- ▶ **How quickly people agree with you compared to normal.**
- ▶ **Whether they start echoing your words or ideas.**

- If they seem more excited or engaged when you reinforce positive anchors.
- If they take action sooner after you introduce emotional urgency.

If something doesn't work, adjust your approach and try again with a different influence technique.

Final Reflection: What You Learned About Influence

At the end of **Day 7**, ask yourself:

- *Which techniques worked best in real life?*
- *Did people react differently when I structured conversations using influence principles?*
- *Did I feel more confident in steering interactions?*

By now, you should have a **clear understanding of how influence works in everyday situations**—and the ability to apply it **whenever you choose**.

Next Steps: Mastering Influence Beyond This Experiment

This seven-day challenge was just **the beginning**. To truly **master influence**, continue practicing these techniques in different areas of life:

- **In Business:** Guide negotiations, sales, and workplace interactions with subtle influence.
- **In Social Settings:** Build deeper connections, lead conversations, and steer group decisions.
- **In Personal Relationships:** Strengthen bonds, defuse conflict, and create positive emotional anchors.

The more you apply these techniques, the more **effortless and natural your ability to influence will become**.

Influence isn't about forcing people to do what you want—it's about shaping reality in a way that makes them want to do it themselves.

Final Thought: The Ethical Use of Influence

With great influence comes **great responsibility**. The techniques in this book can be used to **guide, persuade, and inspire**—or they can be **exploited for manipulation and control**.

The true power of influence lies in **how you choose to use it**. Mastering these techniques will allow you to:

- **Detect and defend against manipulation.**
- **Use persuasion to create win-win outcomes.**
- **Control your own mind while subtly shaping the reality of others.**

Whether you use these skills for **business, relationships, leadership, or personal growth**, the ability to **influence without detection is one of the most powerful tools in the modern world**.

FINAL WORDS
MASTERING INFLUENCE AND PROTECTING YOUR MIND

You have now completed **The 7-Day Influence Experiment**, testing **covert manipulation techniques, psychological persuasion, and emotional influence** in real-life situations.

By this point, you should have **a deeper understanding of how influence operates beneath the surface**—and more importantly, how to **detect and counter it when used against you**.

This final section summarizes the **core lessons** from the book and provides **next steps** to continue refining your mastery of persuasion and mental autonomy.

Key Takeaways: What You Have Learned

Mastering covert influence is about **understanding human psychology** and using it to guide behavior **without triggering resistance**. The five most important lessons from this book are:

1. Perception is Reality – Control the Frame, Control the Outcome

- People do not react to **objective reality**—they react to **how reality is framed**.
- If you control **how a situation is perceived**, you control **how people respond** to it.
- Framing techniques allow you to **steer conversations, decisions, and emotions** in your favor.

How to Apply It:

- Instead of **arguing facts**, reshape how those facts are presented.
- Control **context and narrative**, and people will naturally align with your perspective.

2. Subtlety Wins – Direct Control Triggers Resistance

- Overt manipulation creates **pushback**, while **subtle influence goes undetected**.
- People resist **being told what to do**, but accept **ideas they believe were their own**.
- The most effective persuasion happens **below conscious awareness**.

How to Apply It:

- Use **suggestion instead of commands** (e.g., *"I wonder if this would work..."* instead of *"You should do this."*).
- Plant ideas subtly and **let them take root over time** rather than forcing them.

3. Emotional Control is the Key to Influence and Resistance

- Manipulators exploit **fear, guilt, excitement, and urgency** to override logical thinking.
- If you control your **emotional responses**, you become **immune to psychological influence**.
- Likewise, if you **trigger emotions in others**, you gain the ability to **guide their decisions**.

How to Apply It:

- If someone tries to pressure you, ask: *"Am I feeling this way naturally, or is this emotion being manipulated?"*
- Use **anchoring techniques** to attach positive emotions to your presence or ideas.

4. Repetition and Priming Shape Beliefs

- The brain **accepts repeated information as truth**, even if it is false.
- The first exposure to an idea **primes the mind**, making it more likely to accept it later.
- Small, repeated suggestions **reshape beliefs over time**.

How to Apply It:

- Introduce an idea **casually before making a direct request**.
- Repeat key phrases or concepts in **different contexts** to reinforce their impact.

5. Mental Autonomy is Your Greatest Defense

- The best way to **avoid being manipulated** is to **question everything—especially what feels familiar**.
- Be aware of **your own cognitive biases**—they are the easiest way for others to control you.
- The moment you become **fully conscious of manipulation**, it **loses its power over you**.

How to Apply It:

- Whenever you make a decision, ask:
  - *"Am I choosing this because I truly want to, or because I've been primed to?"*
- Practice **non-reactivity**—delaying emotional responses prevents **impulsive influence**.

How to Continue Mastering Influence

1. Refine Your Awareness of Manipulation in Everyday Life

- **Watch for framing tactics in media and advertising.**
- **Observe social interactions** to see when people subtly steer conversations.
- **Analyze political speeches** for emotional triggers and repetition techniques.

The more you **see manipulation in action**, the more immune you become.

2. Develop Tactical Influence Skills in Conversations

- **Practice mirroring in every interaction.**
- **Use priming techniques** before suggesting an idea.
- **Experiment with different emotional triggers** and see what works best.

By **making these techniques second nature**, you can **influence effortlessly** while remaining in full control of your own thoughts.

3. Train Your Mind to Resist Psychological Influence

- **Limit exposure to algorithm-driven content** (social media and news cycles).
- **Seek multiple perspectives** before accepting any idea as truth.
- **Detach emotionally** from persuasion attempts before making a decision.

The more **mentally independent you become**, the harder it will be for **anyone to manipulate you**.

Final Thought: Mastery of Influence is the Ultimate Power

Influence is the foundation of **social, business, and political power**. Those who **understand** and **apply** these techniques **control reality**—those who remain unaware are simply **controlled by others**.

With the knowledge in this book, you now have the tools to:

- Detect and defend against manipulation.
- Influence others **ethically** and **subtly**.
- Maintain **full autonomy over your thoughts and decisions**.

The choice is now yours:

- Will you apply these techniques for persuasion and leadership?
- Or will you use them defensively to protect yourself?

Either way, you now **see the world for what it truly is**—a battlefield of influence, where those who control perception hold the greatest power.

Next Steps

If this book resonated with you, you're already ahead of the curve. But your journey doesn't stop here.

To go even deeper in building psychological resilience, defending your mind, and understanding the forces that shape human behavior, consider:

- **Exploring the traits and tactics of narcissists and manipulators** in *Trapped by Narcissists*—and how to protect yourself from emotional predators.
- **Uncovering the hidden machinery of mass influence and propaganda** in *The Mind Hijackers*, where you'll learn how beliefs, emotions, and decisions are hijacked on a global scale.
- **Mastering emotional strength and bounce-back power** in *Resilient by Nature*, a guide to regaining control, even after psychological devastation.

Influence is real. Manipulation is everywhere. But with the right awareness, you don't have to be a victim—you can become unshakable.

Enjoyed the Book? Let Others Know.

If The Puppet Master's Playbook gave you new insights or made you see the world differently, I'd truly appreciate it if you took a moment to leave a review on Amazon.

Even a few honest words can make a huge difference—not just for me as the author, but for readers who are searching for exactly what you just found.

Your voice helps others see what's behind the curtain.

Thank you for reading.